Endorsements

"Ms. Danyluk has the heart of God and whose life is built upon the foundation of integrity, character, honesty, and compassion. Mary Jo has a passion for the hurting, neglected, and those that have been tossed upon the junk pile of life and forgotten. She has an anointing for looking into the hearts of people while sensing their hurt and pain. Mary Jo does not judge others from their past, only seeks to assist in helping them discover their destiny and purpose for life. A woman with the heart of God and my friend for life."

~ James J. Washington, Dean of Academic Affairs of ITT Technical Institute

~~~~~~~~~~~~~~

*"Mary Jo has found hope in the only One who can offer true Hope and in that hope comes peace. Through God's grace she has conquered many obstacles including abusive relationships, rejection, abandonment, and even homelessness. As the pages of the book reveal God's grace in the stories she shares, Mary Jo paints a beautiful picture of how she found peace in her pain. Now, she is revealing how you too can find peace in your pain. This book is a tool that can easily be applied to your life whether you are facing a storm or if you have come out on the other side. It is a book of inspiration that will encourage your faith and re-ignite your desire to see God's hand in every minute detail of your life and in a very tangible way. Using the models within the pages of this book will deepen the faith of most anyone. It is my prayer that this book brings others to Christ so that they can truly feel His love for them and they too can find **Peace in their Pain.***"*

~ Angela Hawke, Executive Director of The CARE Center

Endorsements (continued)

"I have known Mary Jo for the past 23 years. I am able to attest to her character being that of the utmost of high morals and values. Mary Jo and I have developed a very deep friendship. I am able to sincerely say that she first and above all else looks out for the best interest of others before herself. She is a warm, sensitive, pleasant person and has a positive outlook on life despite what she may be going through. She treats everyone with courtesy and respect and relates well to people of diverse, socio-economic and cultural backgrounds. She is very intelligent and confident. Her journey through the pain in her life has projected her to the other side, as she now offers hope and healing for others which she has obtained herself. Knowing Peace in the Pain has been possible for her, assures me, others will obtain the same relief she has found."

~**Edna Green-Perry**, Hurley Medical Center, Human Resource
Board Committee

Peace in the Pain

~~~~~

Truth Therapy

A Therapeutic Approach
to the Realness of Life

The Clip

The Button,

and the Jelly Beans

Mary Jo Danyluk, MAC, LLPC

© 2013 Mary Jo Danyluk

Published by:
Zoë Life Publishing
P.O. Box 871066
Canton, MI 48187 USA
www.zoelifepub.com

Author: Mary Jo Danyluk
Cover Art Work: Heather Carney
Editor: Zoe Life Editorial Team

First U.S. Edition 2013, paperback

Publisher's Cataloging-In-Publication Data

Danyluk, Mary Jo

Peace in the Pain

Summary: In this book and through her practice, Mary Jo has discovered the Truth in the application of *Truth Therapy.* She has found that once the victim (the person in emotional pain) discovers, understands and applies the Truth without exceptions, they are set free and even in the midst of their pain, they find peace.

13 Digit ISBN 978-1-938807-50-3 Perfect Bound Softcover

    1.   Devotionals, Christianity, Truth Therapy, Christian Counseling

Library of Congress Control Number: 2013941844

For current information about releases by *Mary Jo Danyluk* or other releases from Zoë Life Publishing, visit our website:
http://www.zoelifepub.com

Printed in the United States of America
v2.3 06032013

The dedication of my life is likewise to Whom
the dedication of every word herein.

~~~~~~~~

You.
You alone have always been…
been there for me.
Alone.
Afraid.
Depressed.
Unsure.
Misunderstood.
Abandoned.
Persecuted.
Ridiculed, and yet…
You have aided me to bear down, endure the pain
and acquire the peace found not elsewhere
as You
and You alone have worked *all* things out for my good
(no exceptions).
Lord, because of Your relentless love for me and the
manner in which You, without ceasing, lavish the realness
of Who You are daily into my life, there is no other to
whom this honor is due

.~~~~~~~~~~

To You alone be the glory for what You have done in my
life
And what You are about to do in each one here.

READING THE
THE STORY BEFORE THE STORIES,
REASONS FOR THE STORIES, THE
PREFACE
AND
INTRODUCTION
ARE
PRECURSORS
TO THE
REMEDY
OF
ACQUIRING
PEACE
IN
THE
PAIN.

Contents

A Story Before The 'Stories'
(the Birth of the Cover)

A friend of mine told me of a Christian Conference. She stated that I *must* attend. Knowing the depth of my friend's relationship with the Lord, and from times past how she has been led to speak other things into my life, I heeded the Lord's instruction through her.

While at the conference I attempted to partake of a few break out sessions; because I had waited to the last minute to decide to attend, they were all full to capacity.

I aimlessly (or so I thought) walked around and chose to (rather was led to) step into the Prayer Room. Upon entering, I sat on the front row and began interceding for my two bosses. I looked up at the easel in front of me; it was supplied with art mediums; produced from them were prayers and poems which filled the space. All of a sudden I saw it, a work of art! I read it and began to weep out loud. "Yes, Lord break their boxes" I cried (pertaining to my bosses' manner of functioning).

Immediately the Lord said to me, "What about your box?" "My box?" I said. "Yes. You have allowed others to place you in a box." Amazingly enough, He was right. (Like He has ever been or ever will be wrong; I know better.)

This epiphany ceased the echo of others opinions to unconsciously become imbedded into and therefore become a part of my identity. This day the repetitive cycle of self-fulfilling prophesies ceased! Now that's God! Now that is the Truth. Truth Therapy…growth!

Knowing the positive or negative repercussions emotionally, from one viewing art in a person's life (as Art Therapy was an elective I chose for my Master Degree program), I felt I 'had' to have a copy of this visual aid to continue the positive effects of it in my life.

I inquired of the leader who sat next to me, "Who drew that work of art? I need to ask if I can make a copy of it. " "Oh, Heather drew that; she's right there. Let me ask her if you can make a copy." Heather would not allow me to make a copy of it; she signed it, turned it over and wrote:

Lord,
We want you to open
our eyes to the possibilities.
We want you to come & move
in such a powerful way
that you would break our boxes.

You can do more than we
could ever think or imagine (Eph. 3:20-21).
We expect you to move & breathe
on us in a new way. We expect
to receive more by Your Spirit.
You are doing a new thing.
Expand your territory through us,
for Your glory! Amen.

She handed it to me and said, "I want you to have it."

Approximately a year later a friend of mine came over and began praying for me. While praying she exclaimed, "Oh my gosh! I just saw the cover of your book; it has all kinds of colors on it." She began to motion with her hand as if it had a paint brush in it, and she were drawing lines and lines of colors. I thought nothing of it until...

I was in my dining room and the Lord said to me, "Look." I looked over and there was what God knew all along would be the cover of this book (Heather's work of art, framed on my wall).

Next task.

Where is this woman (the artist)?

The same friend who suggested I attend the Christian Conference found her through an online, social network.

Heather and I spoke and...brace yourself...

She gave me permission to display the beauty God created through her on the cover of this book.

I stop.

I weep.

I am astonished.

The hand of God and His ability to orchestrate...

Speechless.

Thank you Lord for creating Heather Carney...for such a time as this!

The REAL funny thing is...I had nothing to do with any of this coming about. Clueless is the word. When we have no agenda, He makes things happen that are on *His agenda...not ours!*

Heather Carney has earned a B.S. in Elementary/Middle Education, and is currently working towards a Master's degree in Public Health, Community Health Education. For the past eight years she has served as a missionary in Southern Illinois, taught Junior High Math, and worked with non-profit organizations in various capacities. Her passion for artistic expression was further developed after receiving training at Bethel School of Worship in Redding, California. In all of her pursuits, her desire is to equip and mobilize people in living an abundant life.

Peace in the Pain – Truth Therapy
(a Therapeutic Approach to the Realness of Life)

~~~~~~~~~~~~~~

Where pain is inevitable…

peace is possible.

~~~~~~~~~~~~~~

The Reason for the Stories

God, I made a promise to you that I was to begin the book…the book in which at least 11 people now have told me I need to write…after the 11th person telling me, I chose to FINALLY be obedient.

Sorry God for my disobedience. I forgot all about our date tonight (to begin this endeavor) until my friend said to me, "Mary Jo, you have such a way with words that I have never experienced or heard before, it is like I am living it…what you have experienced. You have a gift to reveal to others something they don't see in themselves. I just pray one day you see the depth of who you are, the depth in which God uses you to meet them and aid them in healing."

So out of obedience here I am not knowing what to say, but being assured that when You, Lord have spoken, I have listened; every time without exception you have shown up in a manner that amazes all, including myself.

You…God in me…it is not me; others who are astonished
stand in awe of Your ability to work through me, just as I stand
in awe of the revealing of Your presence when You work
through others; that is what I hunger for. This is why they are
coming to me for a Word in due season…because it is You in
me…You…the One and Only Who is able to satisfy to the
uttermost…to the uttermost of a degree that is unfathomable!!!

This is it. The question: *What* is it that makes one qualified
to write a book? Max Lucado, Charles Stanley, Dr. Dobson,
Billy Graham and all the others…I have wondered. I have come
to know; undoubtedly that it is not w*hat* is it in them, but rather,
Who is in them. Always and forever I possess the answer…the
One and only variable with no standard deviation…You…Jesus
Christ.

If indeed we who are truly devoted (and truly there are
varying degrees of devotion) really *do* abandon ourselves and
allow You, Lord to come in and reign…then assuredly in You
we do live and move and have our being (Acts 17:28).

They…all the authors mentioned above live and move and
have their being in you, and that is what makes them who they
are as well as who I am…a woman after Your heart; I have
captured it, and my heart is Yours as well.

The call is to abandon "our" manner of functioning (in our
will) for "His" will. And the test is here, now…am I really able

to do all things through Christ who gives me strength (Philippians 4:13)? Rhetorical. Rhetorical.

Today I rest and wait and see as you again do yet another amazing thing that leaves not only me this time but all others whose gaze is here astonished...only for your Glory!! ('Cause it is *still* not about me, and thank God never will be.)

Ready...get set...go God!

Preface

Pain. Just the mention of the word causes many to run. What if perhaps the embracing of pain would drive one to surpass his/her present state of distress into a knowledge and understanding that one would not otherwise come to experience?

What if…just what if this pain would cause each of us to become stronger, wiser and more effective so that others could come to know the depth of what it is meant to bring…an unexplainable, unseen but truly tangible life altering asset in our character?

Ahhhh! Then we would welcome the excruciating…we would look into and beyond the ache that seems to overtake our reason and intellect. We would stop *blaming* God for the circumstance and ask for what He died to give…*wisdom in the pain*, and through that a life more abundant and free. Indeed by attaining this joy unspeakable and full of glory, we arrive at and come to truly know the benefits of the life He died to give us; a life exceedingly and abundantly more than what we could ask, think or imagine (Ephesians 3:20). How you say?

So we begin together…a small part of the whole…a relaying to you of what He has done for me. You see, He not only died to "give" to "me;" He did it for "you." This is the only reason why I am compelled to write. I am compelled to obedience in order to administer to you the remedial solution to the dilemma you are experiencing at this very moment.

To allow the feelings of inadequacy which surface to stifle the will of God in my life (to tell you the stories) would therefore stifle the will of God in your life as well (to hear, to be and to continue to become more…more of who *He* desires you to become). I press onto the mark of the higher calling because I know Whom I have believed and am convinced that He is able to guard what I have entrusted to him until that day (II Timothy 1:12)…and that would be you.

There is a lesson; there is always a lesson to learn…everyday of our lives. Undoubtedly:

> "*Everything* happening great and small is a parable whereby
> God speaks to us, and art of life is to get the message."
>
> (Malcolm Muggeridge)

My prayer has always been and likewise is for you: Lord, give us eyes to sce and ears to hear (Matthew 13:16) what the Spirit is saying. To hear and see, through the eyes of our heavenly Father brings perspective unattainable from any other source, and freedom from *every* ill in life…guaranteed.

In my own personal life (in which you will see written within) and throughout the years I have counseled I have come to assuredly know that our distorted perceptions coupled with our narrow intellect do not see beyond the pain.

This lack of insight projects our lives into a space of disillusionment and discouragement; the result is an immobilization so that we are ineffective to fulfill our passion of purpose that burns within; therefore, our 'reason for being' diminishes…and becomes as smoldering embers.

To re-ignite the hope is to obtain the variable necessary to rekindle what is about to die. The Hope…the One and only Hope is the fact that there is an availability of healing…somewhere and somehow.

Knowing the 'where' and 'how' is what I have found. Every time, without exception, this remedy has been administered, it has brought a resolve (beyond what I ever thought possible). I have come to find there is no standard deviation, and this healing source is available unreservedly to anyone at anytime for the asking.

This entity brings about the presence and administration of a healing balm impossible to acquire elsewhere. It is no secret; although many have a distorted perception of the depth of availability due to experiences in the past which have alienated them from the foundational Truth; the Truth of the character of this person is found in a relationship with Jesus Christ. To prove this: Psalm 147:3 declares, "He heals the brokenhearted and binds up their wounds."

In the past, my heart was broken (just as yours) to a degree that it was literally impossible for me to pick up; the innumerable pieces were scattered to such a lengthy distance that I knew my attempt to search would be feeble and ineffective.

In the pain I found peace.

In the pain the peace brought hope.

Peace and Hope bring about an assurance, and aid us to administer the love we so desperately seek ourselves (even while in what we believe to be unbearable pain). I have come to find I have a story (many) I must tell to the nations; for me to withhold what I believe a cure for your heart would be inhumane.

First and foremost the stories below are all true. They are relayed to you for a two-fold purpose.

One is to inform you that each of the experiences are facts, and from the stories are remedies in which the Lord chose to bring *peace in the pain.*

The second purpose is to prove to you that within our own intellect we lack the wisdom and discernment necessary to process the pain in our lives in order to come out of the excruciating and into the exhilarating.

I have truly learned another Truth which saved my life and will yours as well: The Lord states in Isaiah 55:8 and 9, "For my thoughts are not your thoughts, neither are your ways my ways, as the heavens are higher than the earth, so are my ways higher than your ways and my thoughts than your thoughts."

As a state licensed counselor, the seven years of my academic studies have been the precursor to conceptualize events in others' lives and therapeutically administer appropriate techniques that I would not have otherwise acquired. *However*, without the divine wisdom obtained from the leading of the Holy Spirit through the Lord, I whole-heartedly believe every effort to bring about a healing emotionally and mentally would not only be unethical but in vain as well.

So, I run…continually to the Lord to seek and to understand His ways; within those ways is wisdom which makes perfect sense to Him, but simultaneously are incomprehensible by the means of our own intellect.

~~~~~~~~~~~~~~~~~~~~~~~~~~~~~~~~~~~~~

The entirety of each story presented below is expressed in order for you to see clearly that whenever we go through things in life, especially the events which bring about an inexpressible pain, we are humanly tempted to ask, "*Why?*" For this moment, the presentation of a more thorough question is posed in order to bring a permanent resolve: "*What* is it that you want me to learn, Lord?" *Why* blames. *What* learns.

- ❖ Learning brings an awareness of the Lord's constant and forever care…despite despair.
- ❖ Learning proves His ways and thoughts are higher than ours, and knowing beforehand that His intentions are never to harm us but to give us a hope and a future (Jeremiah 29:11) assures us that, no matter what the next battle looks like, He is faithful to bring about that

good…again and again, and oh….again (forever) (Romans 8:28).

As I contemplate the next step…How? How am I able to explain the intangible…the unseen? And, again, I am enlightened…enlightened. This is it…the manner in which the Lord is to write to you now (I will not assume a false sense of responsibility for what only He is able.).

And so let's go…let's go into the wonder of "Who" He really is; let's see how He will retell the *what* I have *learned* so that you too may come to make applicable His insight and wisdom; the remedy which is undoubtedly higher than ours.

Proverbs 19:8

The one who gets wisdom loves life;

the one who cherishes understanding

will soon prosper.

Introduction

Life happens. Life happens to all who live and breathe, and the not so funny thing is…no one ever knows what it is that life will bring to them. Oh yes, we have our plans; we have our life all mapped out. When and where to go to college, whom we shall marry and so the story goes, and then all of a sudden some "one thing" happens that was not in *our* plan. O.K. I can handle that we say, but then another comes and another and yet another.

And we ask, when will the turn in the tide cease? When will the wonderful assurance of *my* plan come into fruition? The good news is: Perhaps it never will.

If the detours of life were pleasant (in our understanding when they are occurring), I am sure not one of us would mind their intrusion in order to benefit the quality of our life. However, more so than not, the detours come unwanted, throwing us into a whirlwind that seems to never cease no matter our innumerable attempts to quiet the uncontrollable.

And so the question arises. "Do we go *with* the flow or fight against it with all that is in us to such a great degree that to be found dead would mean peace at last?" Ahhhhh…I say, "No."

But that God has a plan. Whether we understand what is happening or not, He has allowed every single thing that has come into your life to make you the most happiest person in the world. Yes, because He is sovereign (has control over all things), but yet we wonder…how will *He* work "this one" out? Was it not said earlier that the Lord's ways and thoughts are higher than ours? (Isaiah 55:9) Yes. Then it is best to stop the drive within us to control the uncontrollable at the inception of the deception (the distorted thought). An attempt to figure out and rationalize an occurrence is oftentimes impossible for man, but only possible with God (Matthew 19:26, Mark 10:27 and Luke 18:27). In an effort to take control over that which is out of our control is to not…

Trust.

Trusting…another Truth…that the Lord has promised to work all things out for our good if we love Him and are called according to His purpose, (Romans 8:28). These words of assurance command the fact that God has our best interest at hand (*in His mighty hand*).

Trust.

Trust in the pain that there is a purpose…because His character is that of Faithful (Lamentations 3:23). Has He been there for you before? I believe He has in more ways than one. Then another fact of this matter remains; He is the same yesterday, today and forever (Hebrews 13:8).

Trust.

Trust births gratitude.

How does one acquire gratitude *in the pain?*

No matter what… "He's got this one." (Whatever the "this one" is.)

The only other choice there is would be to succumb to the questions that come; one after another they come…the questions…more and more which leave us in a state of weariness. No answers, just questions.

The harder we search within our own intellect to understand, to *reason* in order to logically arrive at a remedial conclusion, the further away from the rationale ("His" rationale) we become.

What then does one do? Surrender? Surrender to the aftermath of events that were and still are beyond your control and acknowledge the pain to Christ who has *promised* peace that passes understanding (Philippians 4:7)? Yes. Sensibly yes. He, the Prince of Peace (Isaiah 9:6); He is the only One Who is capable of fulfilling such a promise of peace; to run elsewhere is foolishness*; to abandon the pull to hold onto the pain is to relinquish our control into His.*

Let go.

Let go of "it" (the pain) and reach out to grasp the realness of God's steadfast character and presence; the healing balm of comfort and restoration from the One and Only who is able.

The Pain.

The Peace.

The peace given to me liberally in my pain illuminates the stories below which will turn your heart and many others to the reality of and presence of Hope. Yes, gratitude from my pain is present; the reason is that I may comfort you with the same comfort I myself have received (II Corinthians 1:6). More great news: He is no respecter of persons (Acts 10:34); what He has done for me is also the desire of His heart to heal your heart as well.

The Beginning – The Abuse

<u>The Story</u>

Where did it all begin? I suppose at the beginning.

Growing up in a very dysfunctional family seems to have ever lasting effects; some of which seem to surface without warning. My father's voice rang loud and clear, "You're so stupid and good for nothing; you'll never amount to anything." I can hear the words still…not too often…only when I stretch myself into unknown territory that has never been explored before. Part of the aftermath of abuse is fighting, fighting the lies.

As a woman, other women know the depth of the effects a father has on his daughter, whether healthy or unhealthy. No one, not one knows better than the daughter who I believe innately possesses a yearning from God to please her father. If the father supplies the need of his daughter, by giving her the unconditional love she so deserves, every daughter finds a sense of fulfillment; if not she may continually search elsewhere for what she should have received from her father's role of responsibilities. When this need is supplied then she will more than likely feel fulfilled and not continually yearn...yearn for what she had never received, the love she so deserved.

Growing up or shall I say "surviving" in and through the dysfunction from our families of origin brings a pain that oftentimes we are unaware of as we attempt to live out the life before each of us. The footprints of suppressed pain seem imbedded on our hearts that are not in concrete but rather in the form of a dormancy that seems to surface at any given moment.

I never knew...never that the pain was so deep. The physical, mental and verbal abuse from my father did not only leave scars, but left me bleeding internally. The oozing of the pain presented itself in drug and alcohol use (speed and scotch)...driving on a freeway and wondering why everyone was going the wrong way and thinking, "What a bunch of idiots. I'm outta here;" until the dawn of a day, years later, in which I realized it was my fault that I saw the headlights rather than the tail lights. (In other words, I was going the wrong way.)

And so we continue to attempt to live, in the best and only way that we seem is possible. Marrying a man who pushed me down the stairs when I was three months pregnant (before we were married) made sense to me; it was the norm (the painful norm from the abuse in my childhood).

Divorced and marrying another and another and yet another. Why? I had clean hands and a pure heart...I thought that this is what God wanted. But in all the pain there was a reason; I always asked why, and now I know...ever since I've began to *question* rather than *blame*. "Is there something I need to learn?" I would say so; the only other choice is to continue to function in the same manner and produce the same results.

My Thoughts

To be sick and tired of being sick and tired is a beautiful place to be; it is the manner in which the root in the ground is found unwanted, and evokes the desperation to obtain wisdom and knowledge that we know is not present in ourselves.

I know that it would normally seem common sense to some, some...not all, but oftentimes if we are not taught, we do not learn. If it had not been for a woman named, Edna-Green Perry and God, I would not be where I am today. I attended her women's support group in 1991 and came to learn the "Why" that I did what I did.

Again the abuse I received from my father as a child, unknowingly set me up for a pattern to follow; I *allowed* abusive men to pick me. Also, I repeated the pattern of attempting to gain the love and approval of my father into every single relationship I had with the member of the opposite sex. (In essence I was doing and doing and doing for them to love and accept me rather than just being.) Although not healthy, it was normal in its abnormal sense…it was what I was used to…real comfortable. For we operate in a manner in which we have been programmed (unknowingly I might add).

To think I deserved better was another story. You see for the one who has been told she is stupid and good for nothing her entire life actually becomes the truth to that person; then we live it out…what we believe about ourselves.

Bottom line. If you believe you're a failure then what will you become? Right, a failure. You see this psychological term used to describe this is that you have created a *self-fulfilling prophes*y. You have actually brought into fruition that which you have predicted to come about.

On the other hand if a failure you have been told you are, another manner exists in which you may live…and that would be to live in the Truth (John 8:32 states, that it is the Truth that sets you free.).

Live a lie out (for your detriment).

Live a Truth out (for your benefit, for the betterment of those around you, and for the glory of God).

Choice.

Choose to do different; the conscious choice to choose different will in turn bring about just that, "different."

Another is needed. Another is needed to come to your aid. There is safety in a multitude of counselors (Proverbs 24:6) and where there is no counsel, the people fail; but in the multitude of counselors there is safety (Proverbs 11:4).

God, with the help of Edna as I mentioned above (the facilitator of a women's support group) changed the course of my life which was based on my history rather than that of any other possibility that I was unaware even existed. Many of the other women at the group had been through much of the same; every one of them aided me to come to see myself from the eyes of another…through the eyes of One who has a "true" perspective on our worth; Jesus Christ.

Your Challenge

I can almost guarantee that, somewhere along the road you have traveled, that a lie has been told to you; perhaps unknowingly you have believed it and therefore are living it out…perhaps to this day.

You see, in a certain place, in our subconscious we are walking, talking and being something other than which is in God's perfect plan and purpose for our lives. Jeremiah 29:11 states, "For I know the plans I have for you," declares the Lord, plans to prosper you and not to harm you, plans to give you hope and a future. This my dear is what is designed for us…a means by which we may prosper, have hope and a future.

How?

Glad *you* asked.

We need to ask. Ask the only One who knows how to "get there" (into the future). I have come to know that, John 16:24 may perhaps be the link in which satisfaction is obtainable, "Until now you have not asked for anything in my name. Ask and you will receive, and your joy will be complete." Ask Him if there are any lies that you live…breathing in and out every day. To not ask, is to consciously choose ignorance. Phew! Listen to what happens to those who choose to not ask for wisdom. "My people are destroyed from lack of knowledge" (Hosea 4:6). The success from the wisdom I gained (when I asked) is in the pages below.

His plan.

His wisdom…produces not only peace in the pain, but productivity to move us from (out of) the old and into our destiny (which you will also see in the pages to come).

If I have just told my story and perhaps you are wondering how I have come to know you and have not met you (as your story is perhaps almost a replica of mine or close to it); then now is the time; now is the time to ask the Lord why things *are,* and *how* to do different so that different will come about.

He has the answer for *He is the answer*. I have heard it say, and perhaps you as well have heard the definition of insanity, and that is, "Doing the same thing over and over and expecting a different result." Doing the same thing results in the same thing; doing something different will… guaranteed, bring about different.

Our Prayer

Lord, I am grateful for your love for me. No matter how many times I have messed up you remain the same, steadfast in your love for me. I pray you reveal to me "the Why" I am the way I am, and the Way to do and continually choose to do different according to Your will. Please put others in my life to come alongside me to give me the support, comfort and belief in me even when I possess none of my own. You have said Lord that there is safety in a multitude of counselors (Proverbs 11:13); lead me to those who are safe and sound in your Word to give me wisdom as I continually obtain it from them and your steadfast Truth, Your Word.

We pray in Jesus Name, Amen.

Going Deeper:

For Women:

Always Daddy's Girl

>by H. Norman Wright

Redeeming Our Treasures,

>*Finding Joy in the Shadows of an Abusive Past*

>by Linda Settles, M. A.

For Men:

You Have What it Takes

>by John Eldredge

For Men and Women:

The Trauma Zone, Trusting God for Emotional Healing

>by R. Dandridge Collings, Ph.D.

Feel the Fear and Do it Anyway

>by Susan Jeffers, Ph.D.

Traveling Light, Releasing the Burdens You Were

>*Never Meant to Bear*

>by Max Lucado

Journey of Courage

>by Tammie Hall

Single Parentness and the Fight to Cease "Stupid"

The Story

There it was…overnight; it happened, just like that and I had no control over it.

We were a family: my husband, three girls, ages 8 months, 2 years and 10 years of age. We lived in a beautiful little town, in a beautiful ranch at the end of a dead end street.

Without warning, I woke up as a single parent…with no high school diploma. I attempted to tackle this with the God-given, intrinsic fortitude I had within. I telephoned McDonalds and asked what their rate of pay was. The bottom line, after taxes and a babysitter were paid…$40.00 weekly!!!!

There was no way that the four of us could have survived on a dollar an hour. Sooooooooooooooo, the second attempt to

37

configure a rationale other than that of my own intellect....I went to the Lord.

Out of desperation, I heard His voice loud and clear when I asked His opinion of what I should do; His reply..."You need to go to college." Without a second between his verbalization and my response He heard from me, "You don't understand God, I'm stupid." (I just knew "stupid" didn't do college.) His response to me was very loving but *sternly* spoken, "You heard me." The sternness coupled with His love and His desire to see best for me was from the tone within His heart; it relayed to me, "This is the Way you should go, now walk in it...[now]" (Isaiah 30:21).

The next day I recall standing on a sidewalk, my hand outstretched and so very, very hesitant to 'touch' the door handle of the college. I know me well; I am a committed person and to even touch that handle meant that, "I was in," and what a commitment that would be.

I recall the last and exact words; there were five of them, but they were the five words that changed my life. I said to the Lord, "I'm scared." He said, "I'm right here." At that point I had a greater faith in Him and His ability to see me through than that of my own. And that my dear was the only reason why I did what I did by making contact with that door handle; knowing that He is man of His Word and He would help me to do what He had called me to do.

After ten weeks of juggling three little children, full-time college classes and studying and working part-time...not to mention being fully present for my children (the reading of nightly stories, the home room mom, and walks with the children downtown) I received my grades in the mail.

I opened the envelope and made a deal with God; the deal was that if I placed the sheet of paper with the grades on the fridge and they were there in the morning I would believe it.

First thing in the morning I went to the fridge door...not the coffee pot. There they were...all A's!!! My name in black ink on the white paper proved the prior, irrational, distorted self-perception I had of myself.

The end of *this* story: I thought, "Oh my gosh...if I did it once I bet I could do it again," and that I did. Again and again. I ended up graduating with honors and was the only student out of the whole college, in my field of study, who was teacher-nominated for a special honorary acknowledgment.

My Thoughts

Had I not known beyond a shadow of a doubt that God is faithful, He being right there as my hand was extended in mid space to touch the door of a life changing event, I would not be where I am today (and that you will find out later).

God is love (I John 4:8) and love (true love...His love) never fails (I Corinthians 13:8). His love compels Him to work all things out for our good if we love Him and are called according to His purpose (Romans 8:28).

You see...God is *our God (yours and mine) Who* can not lie (Titus 1:2).

He states that we have been fearfully and wonderfully made (Psalm 139:14). I have come to know that there are times when we are purposely confronted with choices...choices to believe the Truth (what our Heavenly Father *knows* and says about our worth) or the lies (that we have unknowingly subconsciously believed by others; those words are of no merit compared to the words of *our* Almighty). To dismiss the unbelief is to embrace the Truth...Truth Therapy. For, as a man thinks in his heart...so is he (Proverbs 23:7).

Right this second...with this breath and the next you are about to take, you will live out the repercussions of "the choice." When I first became a counselor I thought, "Oh God, the people I can change for the better." I have come to know that the only person who can change anyone is his or her self. The most renowned psychiatrist, psychologist or therapist in the whole world knows that he or she cannot change *one* person. What each professional does know undoubtedly that the insight, wisdom and knowledge gained must cognitively transition into a change of behavior.

So here you go....

Your choice to...

Change.

Only two choices.

Please see. Please see clearly that there, more than likely, is a lie that you are living in right this second. This lie has, in some manner, affected the positioning of your steps to where you are right now.

Please see further. This lie was either told to you by someone or it is a distorted perception that you interpreted by another's action; either way, there is pain and that, coupled with the fallacy has perhaps unknowingly determined *your* steps and not *His*.

You see I had no idea that I really and truly believed I was stupid *until* the day came, without warning, when it was staring me straight in the face...circumstances and a choice.

Franklin D. Roosevelt has stated that, "The only thing we have to fear is fear itself." Why should we fear "fear?" Because this is exactly what Satan 'attempts' to instill in *each* one of us. In 2 Timothy 1:7 it states, "For *God hath not* given us the spirit of fear; but of power, and of love, and of a sound mind."

"Why does Satan set the ambush?" you say. Because he, like God knows there are plans...beautiful plans for your life, and to succumb to the fear is to *immobilize* you so you are *ineffective* for your own good and His glory.

So…fear "fear" so that when it creeps up on you your first response is to run and do "it" anyway (whatever the "it" is that God has for you).

The Challenge

I believe daily God has set before us in some manner Life and Death; He has said to choose Life (Deuteronomy 30:19).

Life is the Truth of God's Word straight from His heart and Death straight from the pit of hell which are the lies of the enemy who by the way is still seeking to kill, steal and destroy (John 10:10). Christ has come that we have life and have it more abundantly (John 10:10). Our choice to 'believe or not believe' the Truth dictates the path we choose to walk in life; the circumstances and opportunities of the journey are of *our* choosing, and they reflect just that…Life or Death…and are followed by blessings or curses (Deuteronomy 30:19).

What is it? What is it that the Lord sees in you that you are unaware of? Perhaps at this very second you know immediately what the fear is that you must overcome in order to press on to the higher calling He has on your life.

On the other hand, ignorance is not bliss and if there is something that is holding you back; you can feel a barrier, invisible as it is but nonetheless evident and constricting. The worst part is you have no insight into the nature of the beast, but there will always be "then suddenly[s]" and that is when the Lord Himself shows up to reveal great and might things we know not (Jeremiah 33:3).

Here He is, as He has promised to never leave us or forsake us; He is willing to give wisdom abundantly to all who ask (James 1:5) as He is desiring to reveal the hidden things of the heart (I Corinthians 4:5).

Oh yes…to the believer in Jesus Christ we are called to walk by faith and not by sight (II Corinthians 5:7). Faith to face the pain, and a Companion to walk the path Who brings Life with Peace…a Peace in the Pain. Ask so that you may receive and lack no good thing (Psalm 34:10). His desires align with yours and that is to give you more than what you could ever think or imagine according to His power at work in us (Ephesians 3:20).

Our Prayer

Dear Lord, I am grateful that when I know not about the things in life that you always and forever will. I am grateful that you know my heart and my desire to do your perfect will. Oftentimes I feel that I attempt to accomplish Your will but that there is something hindering the fruition of *your* plan for my life. It is my desire to align with your desired purpose and plan for my life and that is so that others may come to know the depth of *Your love.* I want to be a vessel to pour You out, over and in others so that they will also be astonished by Your love, and so ultimately they may pour You out and over into others as well. Help me Lord to see the hidden hindrance; the unveiling of everything in me that does not bring You glory or stifles the desires of Your heart being fulfilled in my life and in the lives of others. Use me Lord for Your glory! I live to astonish them as you continually astonish me. In Jesus Name, Amen.

Going Deeper:

For Men and Women:

Fearless

by Max Lucado

Battlefield of the Mind

by Joyce Meyer

The Trauma Zone, Trusting God for Emotional Healing

by R. Danridge Collins, Ph.D.

Journey of Courage

by Tammie Hall

Walking by Faith and Not by Sight
is the Place to Be

<u>The Story</u>

I recall the headlines of a local paper in 1991 or 1992; the summary of the article relayed the economic levels of what monetary value was considered to be high, middle, lower and poverty classes.

As a single parent with no mother, father or other relative to come to my aid, I and my three children were living approximately $10,000.00 *below* the poverty level. This oftentimes presented many occasions to where our provision was never received from my hand but from the One and Only hand who said that *He* would provide for *all* our needs (Philippians 4:19); again undoubtedly we call the Lord Himself faithful (Lamentations 3:23). Time and time and oh time again His character reflects Him being true to His Word; I am sure there is a time or two or more to where you are able to testify to the Truth of God's faithfulness.

Three of the most profound sightings of God's provision for my family, as a single parent, again living $10,000.00 *below* the poverty level are: (1) The day the resource of $2,000.00 was found in my mailbox, (2) the appearance of the toilet paper, and (3) the materialization of brown bags filled with sustenance.

Faithful…as expounded below:

Humility came at the submission of pride; it was the relinquishment of my self-sufficiency. With three children and no means to support them or myself, I succumbed to the state making provision for my family. They paid my house payment, gas and electric and I received food stamps as I embarked on my educational feat; I also received $36.00 every two weeks of cash assistance. The $18.00 a week paid for diapers and gas in my car to get back and forth to college. In essence there was not a penny for property taxes, car insurance, phone bill, and the items that food stamps would not provide such as laundry soap, dish soap, face soap, clothes for the kids, personal items and toilet paper.

I recall picking strawberries for $1.00 an hour and crying with gratitude when they handed me $10.00 so I could buy diapers for my baby and not use the kitchen towels anymore… without plastic pants (Couldn't afford one pair of those…Sorry…the truth!). Because I was unable to pay for the property taxes the day came when a foreclosure notice arrived in my mailbox.

Pain. Inexpressible. Pain…and Peace in it.

I recall the night I cried and told God something He already knew…that I could not, in any way pay for the taxes. I prayed and totally trusted Him with my life and my childrens' lives (and our home). It was not even a week later and my answer appeared in my mailbox! A letter from social services stating that they would pay up to $2,000.00 in back taxes!!! Pain…and more Peace in it. Knowing I was at the end of me, and when we are…there God is! Just because our hands are tied…His are not…EVER!

Prior to the severance of my marriage, my name could have been Solomon; "I wanted…", "I wanted….", and I like him thought "it" (things) would suffice the yearning I never knew that only God could fill. Until the day came when I had a revelation to the fact that I had no toilet paper, and the position I was in when the realization came about…you do not want to know. No matter, as I was in the bathroom crying out to the Lord I said, "All I want is toilet paper." There I was at the end of me and there He stood….faithful (because He is unable to be anything else).

At the end of my cry for help I heard a knock on the front door and left my position in the bathroom to attend to the announcement of someone. I opened the door to see a friend of

mine who lived twenty-five minutes away and would *never*
come without calling first. She had actually never been to my
home before; she was a doctor's wife and a single parent over
night with six children as her husband left her for another
woman. After the shock of seeing her face, I looked at what her
hands were holding...toilet paper!!!! I began to ball (cry) *bawl*
uncontrollably. She said, "What's the matter?" I could not
speak. She continued, "Don't ask me what I'm doing here, all I
know is that you needed toilet paper." She also made mention to
be careful not to throw away the $10.00 bill in the package!

As stated earlier self-sufficiency was worn around my neck
like a boulder (unknowingly to me at the time). Pride has a way
of doing that...possessing it and all along not knowing you're
part of it.

Nonetheless, I recall the evening my children and I had our
last dinner. We had *nothing, absolutely nothing else to eat but
that which was before us on the table.* (At this time I was not
receiving food stamps.) I recall saying, "Girls let's thank God for
our last supper." My 10 year old at the time began crying and
crying (I thought boy did I just make a mistake.). I said, "Honey
are you o.k.?" She said "Yeah mom, we're just having our last
supper like Jesus did with the disciples." It was all could do not
to cry with all that was in me. There it was...peace; peace in the
pain.

When I stated earlier that we had no food, that means that we did not have one can of any kind of food in the cupboard, no milk, bread or *any food at all.* I never told anyone, not one person (that pride again) that we had no food. The very next day when I pulled the car in the garage there were at least 7 brown bags filled with groceries lining the wall of my garage in front of the entry way into our home!

My Thoughts

Amazed you are? I still am; that was at least 20 years ago. God has a way of doing that (if we remain in the attitude of gratitude and faithful to Him). Faith does come by hearing (Romans 10:17); you have heard and I pray it is your faith which has increased. You see we all have stories…beautiful stories to tell to the nations that will turn their heart to the Lord; I would love to hear your story. At the end of the book is an address you may write to and tell me your story; this would be following through with what God Himself has commanded, "Encourage one another in the Lord" (2 Corinthians 13:11, 1 Thessalonians 4:18, 1 Thessalonians 5:11 and Hebrews 3:13).

You see there are times when only God Himself is able to reveal His "bigness" to us to a degree of unfathomable astonishment; then at each recollection of the event, we relive an amazement of the "awe-ness" of His hand…over and over again.

And that my dear is the manner in which we should remain. It is called joy unspeakable and full of glory (I Peter 1:8).

To recall these times past of His provision and/or presence is to assure us that He really is the same this moment (whatever you are going through) and *will* remain the same today, and all our tomorrows.

For He is the One and Only reason why…why we can experience Peace in the Pain.

The Challenge

To believe…to truly believe that because God said that He would be all that we need and so much more…forever (Philippians 4:19) is the reason why….the only reason why we are able to have peace…peace in the pain.

So often I pray like the father of a child in the Bible, Lord, I believe; help my unbelief (Mark 9:24). Whatever the need is right now; perhaps to be loved, to be healed, to be provided for, to experience the nearness of His faithfulness despite "it all." If it *seems* impossible for anyone to work out what you are going through, you are probably right because He is not just anyone. He has said three times in the Bible that what is impossible with man is possible with God (Matthew 19:26, Mark 10:27 and Luke 18:27), and that *all* things are possible to him who believes (Mark 9:23).

If we are called to be *believers,* and that we are…then my dear we are called to *believe*…believe that the same God that was…still is (no matter what). He is the same, same, same… yesterday, today and forever (Hebrews 13:8), and oh yes again and again and again, "Great is His faithfulness" (Lamentations 3:23).

Great news! Our Savior saves, and He is no respecter of persons (Acts 10:34). What He has done for me, and for another He will do for you. To surrender means to lift our hands and hold them high, empty handed so that His will is done, and not what we believe to be the wisely executed plan of our own. And then the peace, yes the peace that passes all understanding, despite the *appearance* of chaos, will guard our hearts and minds in Christ Jesus (Philippians 4:7).

Yes pain. Ohhhhhhhh but yes…peace.

Peace.

Not obtainable elsewhere by any other means.

Choice again.

Where is your gaze? Turning your head will alter your vision, cognition and behavior; bringing into focus the Author and Finisher of your faith (Hebrews 12:2).

Our Prayer

Lord, we pray that no matter what…no matter what God, that You will continue to be the Finisher of our faith, as you have promised that You would. You have said that You have given each one of us a measure of faith (Romans 12:3). You would not ill-equip us with less than what we need…that would be inhumane, and that You are not.

And so we sit or stand or lie down, live, breathe and believe (have faith) that You are ready, willing and very well equipped to move any mighty thing with Your mightier hand in our lives. Aid us to rest in peace while alive. In Jesus Name, Amen.

~~~~~~~~~~~~~~

Question: How big is God?

Answer: Bigger than what you think He is (no matter how big you think He is, He is and will forever remain…bigger).

BY *Mary Jo Danyluk*

Going Deeper:

For Men and Women:

Desperate for Hope
   by Bruce Martin

A Shepherd Looks at Psalm 23
   by Phillip Keller

Dangerous Wonder
   by Michael Yaconelli

Journey of Courage
   by Tammie Hall

The Accident

The Story

The end of the last story resulted in me acquiring my Associate's Degree in Business (3.8 gpa), and then further to receive my Bachelor's in Family Life Education (Psychology) (3.9 gpa); this story, now being told, is the inception of acquiring my Master of Arts in Counseling.

And so the day came in the fall of 2006; the first day of class for my Master's degree. Six days later on October 1, 2006 on the drive to church something else also came. The bang of a noise was something I had never heard before and as I looked up the rear view mirror was nowhere to be found. In an attempt to make sense of it, I looked out the windshield and could not, for the shattering of it would not allow me to find even a peep hole. The spinning of the car in the middle of the road ended up:

- Placing me to not be able to walk on my own for 1-1/2 years,
- Bound to a wheel chair for six months,
- A broken left heel and left collar bone,
- My teenage daughter and I were removed from our home (due to it not being handicap accessible), and placed into a hotel to live, for again approximately six months,
- Timing my pain medication so that I could function to complete my academia for my Master's Degree (I could not type at all due to my broken collar bone); a 51 page paper, typed was due,
- My car being totaled, and the insurance paying me $500.00 for it as I had limited insurance, and
- No job to acquire another car.

BUT GOD:

- Aided me to walk again on my own in a little over 1-1/2 years,
- Provided a buffet breakfast every morning and a buffet dinner 5 days a week at the hotel (and room service I might add...clean sheets and towels every day),
- Provided a friend who is a medical transcriptionist who typed all my papers and emailed them to me as I plucked

away with one hand, making corrections with my index finger (as I could still not move my left shoulder),

♦ Provided an incredible manager of the hotel who allowed me 24 hour access to the vacant office of the assistant general manager (for they were in the process of interviewing for that position),

♦ Allowed my daughter to care for me and was paid by the insurance company to do such; she purchased her first car that we both used until I acquired my own.

♦ Received three years lost wages while I was off work (80% of my income), and most importantly,

♦ Ministered to all who came into the hotel who were homeless due house fires or guests who were there for an out of town funeral. One pastor came in from out of town to interview at a church and lovingly was led by God to give me signed copies of two books he had written.

♦ And to boot it all…I graduated with my Master of Arts in Counseling (3.9 gpa)!

My Thoughts

Oh how man plans his way, but how God orders our steps (Proverbs 16:9).

There is a fine line between planning our life and allowing God to lead. I did plan on acquiring my Master's Degree (as led by the Lord); God ordered my steps and worked not only on my behalf but for the good of others.

Despite the pain (physically) there was peace.

Just knowing that He would follow through as He had promised eased not only the physical pain but the emotional pain as well.

Good news again! He is no respecter of persons (Acts 10:34). What He has done for me, He will do for you in *any and all* situations you are or ever will be in. Only He is able to work *all* things out for our good (Romans 8:28). There are however two conditions in this verse: if you love Him and that you are called according to His purpose (to do what He has for you to do).

Your Challenge

When we step out to do the Lord's will, more often than not we have to believe we can walk on water (walking by faith that is…not by sight). Beware: Someone else will present himself as soon as we step out of the boat, and that would be Satan himself. It is then (as we should everyday) *just believe* in the Lord. Believe that apart from Him we can do nothing (John 15:5). But with Him we can do all things (Philippians 4:13).

Oftentimes we wonder why. We wonder why things happen (*when* they are happening). It is only when "it" (whatever it is) is *over* that we can see the trail of love all along the path behind us, and that the entirety of each maneuver was orchestrated by the precision of His mighty right hand.

And so…what is "it?" There is always, just about every day it seems, to be something that leaves us with no answers to our inquiries.

Just to be as a child of the Lord, with the assurance that our loving and heavenly Father knows best, will bring about just that…His best.

No if's, and's or but's about it…period.

To know Him is to love Him and to love Him is to know Him. If your earthly father was not there for you as mine wasn't, don't worry. God looks nothing like your father (inside or out). He is worthy to be trusted; for His character is undaunted…flawless. He is God who cannot lie (Titus 1:2); a*ll…every one* of His promises are Yes and Amen (2 Corinthians 1:20).

Our Prayer

Dear Father, I do not understand what is happening in my life right now. You already know that the desire of my heart is to trust in you; help me to not lean on my own understanding, but in all my ways acknowledge you as I *allow* You to direct my path (Proverbs 3:5-6). You Lord have parted the Red Sea. You have raised people from the dead. You are wise and big enough to handle what I am entrusting to you this day. I believe, Lord help my unbelief (Mark 9:24). In Jesus Name, Amen.

Going Deeper:

For Men and Women:

Crazy Love, Overwhelmed by a Relentless God
    by Francis Chan
The God Chasers
    by Tommy Tenney
It's Not About Me
    by Max Lucado

The Clip

<u>The Story</u>

I will never forget the day…the day the story of "The Clip" was told by my pastor because it has aided me to look for more "clip like" happenings since that day. And the story is… (told to the congregation on a Sunday morning) as follows:

Pastor said that he was out of town preaching and it was time for him to come home. He stated that whenever he was to come home from being away, he and his wife would dress up as they met each other at the airport. He said he recalled looking at himself in the mirror and thinking, "You sure are good lookin'." And then he saw what he believed to be a flaw in his character…a worldly imperfection that marred his desired presentation of himself to his wife. It was nothing other than his "clip." The *grey* clip which held his *black* phone. His gaze at the

61

scenario required an immediacy of prayer… "Lord, I wish I had a black clip to go with my black phone."

While at the airport, waiting for his flight he buried his head in a newspaper. A gentleman came up to him and said, "I see you have a *black* phone and a *grey* clip." Pastor stated to the congregation that he now knew that he was not the only one who understood the depth of his despair. He stated that for a moment he was even embarrassed. The man went on… "I see you have the same phone I have; my phone is *grey* and I have a *black* clip; do you want to trade clips?"

My Thoughts

There is nothing (other than his wife's presence) that could have made his day; for you see…the presence of God prevailed. God totally heard the depth of his prayer prior to leaving the hotel ("Lord, I wish I had a black clip to go with my black phone").

Perhaps I can hear one of you saying, "Yeah, yeah…sure. Is God really concerned about a clip and a phone?"

Our God desires to bestow blessings on us; the question is, "Why?" Perhaps His purpose is two-fold: to "knock our socks off" but more importantly so we will tell the story to others so that they can hear, see and come to experience the ever present realness of our God. Why? So they in turn can tell others (you are one of the others). Yes we do have a story to tell to the nations that will turn their hearts to the Lord. I believe....I believe whole heartedly that God is true to His word...that He is no respecter of persons, and what He has done for Pastor Jim, He would do for me (and for you too). And He did it for me in ....The Button (the next story)...

Your Challenge

Pray and *ask* the Lord to give you eyes to see and ears to hear what the Spirit is saying, and watch, wait and see...You will be presented with an astonishment of God's hand to where you must....are *compelled* to tell another...many others.

The realness of a real God is really real in our lives every day, and to live for the sightings of His hand to be revealed is a life lived in love for Him. As we see His love for us unfold, and for so many others it is because it's really not about you and me but you know Who.

Our Prayer

Lord, the only desire of my heart is to experience the realness of Who You are, and to have others come to that same realization. We ask that you reveal yourself in a real way not only to us, but to others so that we will all stand in awe...astonished...by and for Your glory!

In Jesus Name, Amen.

Going Deeper:

For Men and Women:

It's Not About Me

by Max Lucado

Crazy Love, Overwhelmed by a Relentless God

by Francis Chan

Dangerous Wonder

by Michael Yaconelli

The Button

<u>The Story</u>

So if you are still questioning *The Clip* story let me enlighten you to *The Button*.

As stated earlier I was compensated monetarily for pain and suffering from the car accident. How God worked the accident out for my good still resonates with gratitude. I was able to purchase a one-year old car and place half the cost as a down payment. Never could I have imagined owning such a beautiful car. Gratitude. Until that is, when I noticed something strange in the dead of the night.

As I was driving I noticed on my dashboard a "very bright light" which shone through one of the buttons more so than through the other buttons; it was the on/off button for the stereo. Because it had been pushed on and off so many times the black part of the button was scratched off more than it should have been...normal wear and tear.

Normal? I did not like this normal; others asked me what was wrong with that same specific button (so I knew this was not my normal bit of Obsessive Compulsive Disorder tendencies).

I found myself complaining out loud. Yes it is alright to talk to yourself. One of my professors stated that it is even better if you answer yourself, because verbalizing your thoughts aids your decision-making (*Be careful where you do this though!*). I said, "That button looks so horrible God, I wish I had another button." The audacity for me to complain to God about a button when He had spared our lives and provided a beautiful car for me to drive. I repented for complaining and sincerely forgot all about the button until....

One day as I was driving to my surgeon's office, I was listening to a CD in my car. When I finished my appointment and started the car, the CD player should have begun to play automatically; it did not. I ejected it and placed it back into the CD player; every feeble attempt to remedy the dilemma left me complaining..."God, this is almost a brand new car and the CD player is broken? It will probably cost over $1,000.00 to fix it as this unit is so complex."

I took the car to the dealer, and waited and waited...and waited even more. Finally the clerk said, "I am so sorry Ms. Danyluk but the whole unit of your CD player needs to be replaced. The good news is, it is still under warranty and there will be no charge to you." Relief is not spelled, ROLAIDS; it is spelled FREE!

I am a little slow at catching onto things sometimes; anyone who truly knows me knows this to be true. A couple days later as I was driving in the dark, I noticed something that God did before my very eyes...unknowingly I might add. Yes, my pastor has a new clip and I HAVE A BRAND NEW BUTTON!!!!!

My Thoughts

Is God concerned about even the silly little things that concern us? You bet He is, and He will do whatever it takes to prove He is near with His love that does nothing less than lavish and astonish. "See what great love the Father has lavished on us, that we should be called children of God! And that is what we are! The reason the world does not know us is that it did not know him" (I John 3:1). You see, I believe that God Himself is the Rewarder of those who diligently seek Him (Hebrews 11:1). The Truth. You cannot deny the substantiated Truth. I sought Him and He rewarded me for He is a Man of His Word; he can not lie (Titus 1:2).

I am not saying that every little whim that we desire He brings about. What I am saying is, that the Lord knows *when* we seek Him and *why* we do as well. If we seek him for our own ulterior motives (for His hand and what we can receive, rather than His will) then we will never be astonished by the true rewards for seeking His face. Our focus should always and forever be what He Himself has stated in Matthew 6:33, Seek ye first the kingdom of God and His righteousness, and then all these things will be added unto you. In essence our gaze should be on the desires of *His* heart and He will give us the desires of *our* heart as well. Psalm 37:4 confirms this, "Delight yourself in the LORD and he will give you the desires of your heart."

Your Challenge

Seeking first the kingdom of God requires obedience to what we know we should do (according to the Word). Oftentimes people live any way they want apart from the Lord's desires for them to live, and then expect to be blessed (rewarded with things like "buttons and clips"). Wait until you hear the Jelly Beans story.

For instance, Malachi 3:10-12 declares, "Bring ye all the tithes into the storehouse, that there may be meat in mine house, and prove me now herewith, saith the LORD of hosts, if I will not open you the windows of heaven, and pour you out a blessing, that there shall not be room enough to receive it." Phew!

Requirements.

Requirements for the reward from the One and Only Rewarder.

I suppose the question at hand is…do we desire to please the Lord because we *have to* (in order to 'be' rewarded) or because we *want to* (out of our true love for Him)? I can't answer that for anyone. What was your answer? I Samuel 15:22 states that obedience is better than sacrifice.

His love compels Him to bless us; should not our love for Him compel us to bless Him? (Phew…that was good! Ya know that was God!)

Our Prayer

Lord, we thank you that you test the heart and that what we give to you we give willingly and with honest intent (1 Chronicles 29:17) with no other intent to receive *from* you but to give so that others may come to know the depth of your heart. Sometimes Lord, we have our own agenda and are concerned about things that are of no importance to you; help us to be mindful to prioritize the things in our lives as you would. You Lord were about your Father's business; help us to become even more like you and realize that if we take care of your business…you will take care of ours.

Thank you Lord for concerning Yourself with the things that are often sometimes silly things that may sometimes consume us, and the fact that you even come through to provide the "silly meaningless" is just for You to prove your love for us. Thanking you with more that is in me. In Jesus Name, Amen.

Going Deeper:

For Men and Women:

Crazy Love, Overwhelmed by a Relentless God
    by Frances Chan
God's Favorite House, If You Build It,
  He Will Come
    by Tommy Tenney

I Missed It

The leaves…the leaves…the colored leaves—where did they go? The colors on the leaves in Michigan during the fall season are during a small window of time. As I drive I wonder, "Where are the leaves?" Did I really miss what I long to see every year come to pass before my eyes? I did.

<u>My Thoughts</u>

This causes me to wonder, "What else have I missed?" Was there one who needed a dose of the healing balm of Jesus Christ that I passed due to my preoccupation with self? And I say…

I have not arrived.

I have not arrived.

I have still not arrived.

But I know that I know (meta-cognition) that I've climbed a little higher and walked a little further on the path the Lord has laid before me.

The question is how high is the rung on the ladder in which we are standing? How deep are we in our relationship with Christ; are we so deep that we are over our heads? We should be.

The truth of the matter is, I personally believe we will never arrive at our optimum ability to be healthy mentally. So...why try to reach a point that is impossible to obtain until we are complete on the day we are absent in the body and present with the Lord (in heaven)? Have we missed something in our lives that would have blessed us to the same degree that it would have benefited another, let alone bless our Savior's heart?

To walk in the Spirit is to have eyes to see and ears to hear what the Holy Spirit is saying; then and only then will we live and move and have our being in Him (Acts 17:28). The unseen to our natural eye is thereby seen and brought about as we fulfill the desires of our Lord's heart. This would further aid us to do likewise as Jesus did: To do the will of our Father who as He sent Jesus (John 6:38) also sends us.

I am reminded of my life's mission statement, composed while in my undergraduate work (as follows):

My purpose is to love God with every breath
to a never-ending degree,

72

to daily allow myself to be pliable
so He is effortlessly able to mold me into His image,
to display my love for others
by fulfilling His desire to demonstrate that love,
and to daily live and breathe the breath of life
so others will hunger and thirst after what is in me-
Him
Him alone
Only for HIS Glory!
(11-5-2004)

Our Prayer

Lord, help us to see clearly the items on Your agenda. Take away the clutter and the clamor of the distractions that would lessen our walk with You. To see things accomplished by Your hand is to astonish us in our hearts and those whom are of the same importance to you. To surrender a little more of who we are is to gain so much more of You; then they (those whom you send to us who so desperately need You) will see *You* clearly in us. When they do, they too will hunger and thirst after what is in us…Your righteousness…for then they and we will be filled (Matthew 5:6). Help the desires of our hearts to align with *Your* will on *Your* heart. In Jesus Name, Amen.

Going Deeper:

For Men and Women:

It's Not About Me

    by Max Lucado

Enjoying Where You are

    on the Way toWhere You are Going

    by Joyce Meyer

I Remember

<u>The Story</u>

When I was growing up I recall my mother standing at my bedroom door screaming to my father, "That's enough." The beatings would end at the moment he heard her voice.

Would peace in this pain ever come?

Forever I wondered.

My heart hurt and could not understand the same.

Suffering led to more suffering as I continually lived and yearned for my father's love and acceptance. I would do *anything* in an effort to obtain his approval. "Can I get you a coffee Dad?" "Look at my grades Dad." Not one attempt broke him so I could receive the one thing I needed and never acquired…approval.

Little did I know that this addiction to approval would infiltrate in *every* relationship I would ever encounter for the next 30 or so years! (especially with members of the opposite sex). I did and did and did and did until I could not "did" anymore. Until…I ended up attending a woman's support group in 1992. What I learned in the next 12-15 years is who I am today. Mostly I have learned that love is a choice (pertaining to loving another of the opposite sex) rather than a compulsion to fulfill a huge and gaping wound.

I recall the leader drilling into our heads when, "People say, 'I fell in love.' Whenever I fall, it's by accident, love is a choice." There were mistakes to come; yet to never cease striving to become better is to live better; the better is here, and the best of the better is even yet to come.

To close the story, I ended up reading a book recommended by the leader, "*Always Daddy's Girl*" by Norman Wright. Toward the end of the book, the author challenges the reader to lovingly confront her father with the manner in which she felt as she was growing up. He further went on to say that if your father is dead to write a letter to him and pretend that he is sitting across from you as you read it out loud. Personally, I could not see the latter coming about. I wanted the real deal (confronting him lovingly while he was alive). I know that there are times when a woman's father is no longer alive and the former would be just as effective; but, my father was alive and I was not well.

The day came when I embarked on the first time I ever spoke to my father (implementing the recommendation as stated above). I was so nervous as I had never spoke to my father before (I was approximately 32 years old). He was even more nervous than myself.

I began the conversation by telling him that I had finally read a book for the first time cover to cover. I showed him the book and told him that I thought it was always Mom who had an influence on what kind of woman I would become. I told him that I learned that it was a father/daughter relationship that has the most profound effect on a woman. I further told him that all I tried to do as I was growing up was to get him to love me, and then I did it…I looked into his eyes, so lovingly and said, "Dad, do you hate me?" He said, "No, I love you." No more had to be said…ever.

I ended up being given the honor of taking care of my father for 3 to 4 months after his hospitalization. Making him breakfast, lunch and dinner; seeing his face first thing in the morning and the last thing at night is what I will forever cherish; it all happened because…

Forgiveness had come and love had won.

My Thoughts

I believe maturity in life comes when we realize that our parents were and perhaps may still remain a product of their environment (just as we are to some degree). Not in any manner to excuse abuse, but to truly see the fallen human race as it has always been (and for that matter will always be).

To see that truth eases the pain (not excuses the behavior).

The truth: My father was a military policeman in World War II. The only time I ever heard him speak of the military was when my husband (at the time) spoke of his experience in Vietnam. While he relayed the trauma of Vietnam, my father verbalized (perhaps for the first time in his life) the aftermath of living alive in the effects of his own war (fought on foot and daily fighting the battle within). He said he recalled, as a military policeman having to go into an area which was bombed...the aftermath...the children...the nuns...destroyed.

Now. Now *my* perspective changed. My father was no longer a victim in my eyes but a hero. For me to be aware of what my father experienced...would I not be the same if it had been me? I believe I would be; perhaps even to a greater degree of pain.

But the peace came.

The peace in the pain came...for all.

The facts remain: He said, "I love you." I forgave him.

Peace was forged despite the birth of pain so long ago.

<u>Your Challenge</u>

Assuredly, just as your parent(s) may have imposed suffering in some manner to your life, realistically you have more than likely imposed some degree of imperfection on the children the Lord so lovingly placed in your care.

Perfection will come (in us and in others)...not here, but rather when we arrive at our final destination (to those who are in Christ Jesus).

No matter the manner in which the infliction of pain has come; the remedy lies within.

Jesus Christ.

He has stated that He will show you great and mighty things you know not (Jeremiah 33:3). There is, unquestionably, a resolve. The resolve is found in the Truth

The Truth:

- ♦ When the righteous cry for help, the Lord hears and delivers them out of all their troubles. The Lord is near to the brokenhearted and saves the crushed in spirit (Psalm 34:17-18).

- ♦ He heals the brokenhearted and binds up their wounds (Psalm 147:3).

- ♦ Fear not, for I am with you; be not dismayed, for I am your God; I will strengthen you, I will help you, I will uphold you with my righteous right hand (Isaiah 41:10).

<u>Our Prayer</u>

Lord, I thank you for Who You are. That nothing can separate us from Your love (Romans 8:39). Please Lord, aid me to not allow others who have hurt me to be 'bittermakers' in my life. Please Lord, I pray You give me wisdom so that I may bring a resolve to matters that have caused such great pain in my life. You Lord are the Prince of Peace (Isaiah 9:6); only in You am I able to obtain peace; this is what no other possesses. Please speak to me and show me great and mighty things I know not, in order to bring a resolve that no other is capable of ending. The people who have hurt me…Lord, I pray You convict their heart of the wrong doing. In the meantime please give me the perseverance necessary to do your will. You have said that if I take care of Your business that You will take care of mine (Matthew 6:33). In this moment and in all my moments to come aid me to experience what You died to give to me…peace in my pain. In Jesus Name, Amen.

Going Deeper:

For Women:

Always Daddy's Girl

    by H. Norman Wright

For Men:

You Have What it Takes

    by John Eldredge

For Men and Women:

Desperate for Hope

    by Bruce Martin

Traveling Light, Releasing the Burdens You Were

    Never Meant to Bear

    by Max Lucado

Approval Addiction, Overcoming Your Need to Please

    Everyone

    by Joyce Meyer

The Trauma Zone, Trusting God for Emotional Healing

    by R. Dandridge Collings, Ph.D.

Redeeming Our Treasures,

    Finding Joy in the Shadows of an Abusive Past

    by Linda Settles, M. A.

Journey of Courage

    by Tammie Hall

I Saw a Rock Melt Today
and Another Speak after Eight Months
of being Mute

The Two Stories (same remedy)

For over two years I was a mental health therapist in a correctional facility (in one of the most violent cities in America). Never had I came in contact with a person who did not end up trusting me with his/her life except this one man. His anger and pain were frozen on his face. I never looked at his teeth, but I am guessing he must have gritted his teeth down to his gums as his anger manifested itself in the manner in which his jaw was clenched.

However, I saw…right before my eyes, his hard-as-a-rock demeanor melt as he could not resist the effect of my fervent prayer on his life; as the tenseness disappeared a smile broke out at the same time his eyes lit up (You had to be there!). This man came up to me and thanked me for being there for group therapy.

Another story. I always told my boss, "I want the hardest of the hard inmates to deal with." I had no idea that the one I was about to see was one in which she took me up on my word. I entered the area where the inmate was; the deputy said to me, "You're not gonna get him to talk; the full-time social worker can't even get him to talk." I looked at that deputy and said, "Oh yes I will." See I knew God and I knew that He was always able to do the impossible and that is what I based my assurance.

I sat down to speak with this inmate and tried every therapeutic approach possible; he would not budge *at all*.

Finally I had given up (on my ability to move his mouth and hence hear words from it).

I bowed my head and silently prayed to myself, "Lord, I can't help this man; I pray you help him to talk."

I lifted my head and said to this man, *"I just prayed for you."*

He looked at me. His eyes lit up as he smiled from ear to ear and exclaimed, *"Jesus died for my sins!"*

We talked and talked; I was able to gather enough data to assess and implement therapeutic interventions in order to aid in healing this man. Yes. Jesus saved this man's life way more than once.

When I was walking out of the area the deputy said, "How did you do that? The full-time social worker has been trying to get him to talk for eight months."

I told him I had nothing to do with it; I relayed the true story of how *God* had answered my prayer. The Truth. The peace even this man experienced in his own pain.

My Thoughts

At the end of us…there God is!

What is impossible with man is possible with God (Luke 18:27). Seeing this lived out compels me to know better next time…that there are things that need to be changed in individuals that are impossible for man to accomplish, but ahhhhhh…God! Doing the impossible is what He is all about. Is this not what He did as He walked on the ground your shoes are treading? Wait a minute. I have the answer to that one! Undoubtedly…Yes!

Assuredly, oftentimes we have not because we ask not (James 4:2).

I don't know about you, but I do not want to lack something just because I neglected to ask!

Your Challenge

Perhaps you have a story; more than likely every single person reading this probably has a story about another individual who is in need of change (perhaps even yourself). The change in this person would not only benefit you, but also his/her self and all those whom he or she comes in contact with.

Again, at the end of us...there God is.

Albert Einstein has said the definition of insanity is doing the same thing over and over again and expecting a different result. I have seen parents repeat the same pattern in rescuing their drug addicted child, and I, 100% of the time, predict the outcome...the same thing (so therefore, their child's addiction remains). In correlation to this...if you keep putting oil in your gas tank, I guarantee...yes even stake my life that this in and of itself will not fix the problem. I say...insanity (and know you agree).

So if we know beyond a shadow of a doubt that putting oil in the gas tank does not, and will never work then why do we keep doing it over and over again in the anticipation of expecting the car to start when we turn the key? Good question; I'm glad you asked (Oh that was me who asked, but hopefully you're asking the same.).

In the instance of one of my friends, I believe fear is prevalent. The presence of the fear presents itself at the onset of just *thinking* about doing something different. This fear not only pushes away the alternative in *thinking* but also therefore binds the possibility of changing a *behavior* for the fear of the unknown.

The remedy; for there always is one to any and all dilemmas. I believe the answer lies in the Way, the Truth and the Life (John 14:6). The Lord Himself stated that He would show us great and mighty things we know not (Jeremiah 33:3); remember, to not ask is to not receive (Matthew 7:7); when we ask for wisdom the Lord said that he would give it generously to all without finding fault (James 1:5). The result of not asking is for people to perish from a lack of knowledge (Hosea 4:6) (the only other alternative). Now that is it...therapy...Truth Therapy (based on the only Truth there is...the Word of God).

Asking the Lord for *His* divine intervention is the manner in which dysfunctional behaviors are changed. *Doing different* ceases insanity; it allows God to do what is impossible within ourselves.

Our Prayer

Lord, we ask that you show us *our* part in functioning within *our own* capacity in order to bring about a change either in our self or in the life of another. We have seen you do the impossible at other times in our lives.

You are ready, willing and more than able to bring about what is impossible with man. We are asking that You do whatever it takes to bring about Your perfect will in our lives and in the life of_____(say person's name in which you desire change). You died Lord so that we could have life and life more abundantly (John 10:10). Only You Lord are able to do "…exceeding and abundantly above all that we could ask or think" (Ephesians 3:20).

We believe the Truth (of Your Word), and in the Truth there is peace in the pain. For it is the Truth that sets us free (John 8:32) to experience the peace that passes all understanding (Philippians 4:7). Simple. Hard, but simple.

Oh Lord, You must become greater; I must become less (John 3:30). You have said, "…For it is the one who is least among you all who is the greatest," (Luke 9:48) because it allows you to become all You are *through* us. The cry of our heart aligns with Your desire for each one of us. In Jesus Name, Amen.

<u>Going Deeper:</u>

For Men and Women:

Changes that Heal (book and workbook)
   by Dr. Henry Cloud

Strengths Finder 2.0
   by Tom Rath

The Leadership Secrets of Jesus
   by Mike Murdock

Cheerios® in My Coffee

<u>The Story</u>

Brace yourself. What you are about to hear you may not understand. If I initially inform you that each one of us has a purpose in life and a *driving passion* to "live in" then, understandably so, we are created to bring about a good through divinely created purpose.

As stated earlier in my mission statement it is my (and, oops should be our...sorry, the truth again) desire to live and breathe the breath of life so that others hunger and thirst after what is in us...Him (the Lord)...only for His glory.

So, here it is. My passion is to be in front of the hardest, most volatile criminal. I have come to know that there is no heart too hard in which the Lord is not able to penetrate...ever! He has 100% percent of the time performed the miraculous as I, as well as the offender, both sit in the astonishment of what only He is able to embellish (make beautiful). Totally.

Here is the story: Can you just guess who was the first one to stand in a church, after the announcement was made to sign up for a mission trip to the Ohio State Prison? Certainly you have the answer!

When the day came, our church poured out at least four services at the Prison. Hundreds and hundreds of inmates were set free; those who were held captive behind bars (some for the rest of their lives) were unchained emotionally, mentally and spiritually…right before our very eyes. The weeping, the sincerity of their hearts.

As I relive this moment, I am not here (where I am physically) but am emotionally, mentally and spiritually still encountering that day.

Then the moment came…the Cheerios.

We had a break and ended up being given the honor of eating with and in the presence of the inmates. A man from my church and I sat with a "free" prisoner. While these men conversed, I noticed objects floating in my coffee. Initially they were unwelcomed. As I stared at these little Cheerios, the Lord said to me, "What matters? Does this really matter?" I grew that day; I drank my coffee and the Cheerios at the same time, from the same cup…all the while experiencing the honor.

My Thoughts

The enemy is intimacy is irresponsibility.

Mary chose to sit at Jesus' feet and experience His love like no other, rather than 'attend to' the housekeeping of her guests like her sister Martha chose (Luke 10:38-42). Martha complained to Jesus regarding the humble positioning of her sister at His feet. His response to her *own* dilemma was, "Martha, Martha, thou art careful and troubled about many things: But one thing is needful: and Mary hath chosen that good part, which shall not be taken away from her" (Luke 10: 41-42).

I chose the "...good part which shall not be taken away from [me]" (Luke 10: 42). I still possess it; it has not, and will never be taken away from me...the memory of the moment.

I chose to sit humbly so as not to miss one breath or word spoken by or through the men (and God Himself) before me; I chose the "good part" rather than to care more about the housekeeping task (of those little Cheerios).

I drank the cup set before me and was poured out as a drink offering simultaneously.

If you were to ask any of the inmates that surrendered their lives to Christ that day if peace is possible in their pain, the answer, hands down, would be a resounding, "Yes." As a matter of fact the inmate we sat and ate with was at peace knowing he would never experience walking away from the repercussions of his poor choice; yes, he was a "lifer." Proving his peace that passes all understanding is the manner in which he verbalized the astounding goodness of the Lord and how he was looking forward to walking out all his days as never before (chained but free).

Your Challenge

Those who are my closest friends know I do not always make the right choices; this day I did.

Fact: There are more. There are so many more! They are everywhere! Everywhere we go (Luke 10:2). Every single person we see is in pain...guaranteed. Because if one is breathing...life is happening. If life is happening, there is imperfection and stemming from that breads pain.

Here you go: Would you just walk past one who is, very visually having a heart attack? I can answer that one for you. "No." If you could not help them, you would find another who could.

With that in mind, there are a few facts: Jesus "...went about doing good...and healing all that were oppressed of the devil; for God was with him" (Acts 10:38) and that we are to do likewise (Luke 3:11). Further, it is possible to "Let this mind be in you, which was also in Christ Jesus" (Philippians 2:5) because He would never tell us to have the mind of Christ Jesus if it were not possible.

Last thought, "Why would we not save another's life?" I can't answer that one. (Not in any way condemning...but rather thought provoking... challenging).

Our Prayer

Lord, I am so grateful that each and every one of us that *has* ever lived, *is* or *will ever* be born, was, is or will be (very nonprofessionally speaking) "screwed up." Knowing we will never reach perfection on earth does not give us the rationale to not attempt to be "...changed into the same image [of Christ] from glory to glory, even as by the Spirit of the Lord" (II Corinthians 3:18). Thank you Lord for loving me, totally and unconditionally with this breath I am taking, and each next breath which You so lovingly provide. Please, Lord give us eyes to see and ears to hear what the Spirit is saying; as we go about doing *Your* business may we likewise go about doing *ours* (as You stated, "I must be about My Father's business" in Luke 2:49). You also stated that if we take care of Your business that You will take care of our business (Matthew 6:33).

Help our heart to be committed to You as You aid us to heal the brokenhearted (Luke 4:18) only for Your glory. In Jesus Name, Amen.

Going Deeper:

For Men and Women:

It's Not About Me
    by Max Lucado
Growing Strong in the Seasons of Life
    by Charles R. Swindoll

Do We Walk with Sight and See Blindly?

<u>The Story</u>

Waking up this morning I assumed when my alarm stated it was 8:00 a.m. that indeed it was, but I neglected to "Spring ahead" an hour which made me an hour late for church...or was it that I indeed arrived in perfect time (God's timing)?

I parked (not knowing I was late) and approached the doors to the church.

A young man approximately 21 years of age asked me if I had a light for his cigarette. I said, "I'm so sorry I don't, but I think I have one in my car;" he followed me as I searched diligently in the glove compartment to no avail. Beyond a shadow of a doubt I heard God say, "Tell him to get in the car and buy him a lighter." *Immediately,* without hesitation, I did what I was instructed to do (For far too many years, in the past, when what seemed "the insensible" occurred, I rationalized that it was not God, and that it was I that was 'off the wall.'). When it was disobedience I chose in times past, it was not only I who totally missed God, so did the one He "attempted" to minister to…through me. This time, without skipping a beat…*this time* I was obedient; he hopped in the car and we drove off.

This young man began immediately relaying to me how he was praying and praying to quit smoking; I told him I had a story, a story to tell him how God delivered me from smoking. He said, "I have a story too." He began to deliver it.

He began, "Last week was my first time here; there was a man named Tony and he prayed with me at the altar. I was delivered that day from heroin. You have no idea how much heroin I sold, and how many have died because of me; many of my friends have died because of me giving them what killed them."

He went on further, "Ever since I surrendered my life to God last week, I have not wanted to use at all. I got a job in the morning and another to work at night. I got my income tax refund of $1,700.00, and I am using that for a place to live."

We arrived at the store; I bought a lighter for a man to smoke his cigarettes. (Can hardly believe I said that.)

Upon arriving back at the church he asked if I knew of any meetings that he could attend. I said, "I'm gonna hook you up!" You see God has placed so many recovering people in my life and directors of rehabilitation support groups...for such a time as this (and all the times to come). I gave him my card and told him to call me. I stated that I would attend each of the groups the first time with him so that he would be more comfortable and also so that I could introduce him to many mentors that could love him from darkness into the Light.

My Thoughts

When you deepen your relationship with the Lord, and ask Him to give you eyes to see and ears to hear what the Spirit is saying...WATCH OUT!

What will happen is what you will never expect. Having ears to hear and eyes to see what the Spirit is saying requires a heart of obedience, despite the true fact that what you have heard does not make sense. You see, I would have normally *never* have bought anyone a lighter for his/her cigarettes...but God.

God has a way of revealing Himself in a manner that the person we have come in contact with *needs.* You see, it was NOT the lighter he needed; it was a portion of the love of God in me that he was hungering for, and God Himself supplied that need. Oh yes how God's ways are indeed higher than our ways and His thoughts are higher than ours; who can understand them (Isaiah 55:9)? Not me; perhaps you either. I believe there is one fact that remains; God truly knows what He is doing, and that we do not.

Your Challenge

To not be obedient is disobedience (whether it makes sense or not).

Pray. Ask the Lord to use you, and give you eyes to see and ears to hear what the Spirit is saying. When He speaks and gives you the orders to embark on a journey, pray also that you have a heart of obedience to heed His call on your life; for it is His desire to save many *through* you.

I believe oftentimes it is our fear that stifles the miraculous from coming about. Fear has been said to be an acronym for **F**alse **E**vidence **A**ppearing **R**eal. God has not given us a spirit of fear, but of love, power and a sound mind (II Timothy 1:7). So, common sense tell us that if God has not given us this spirit of fear that there is only one other from whom it comes, and that would be…you know who…Satan himself.

I recall specifically the Lord telling me precisely why Satan does this (causing a spirit of fear). He does it for one purpose; to immobilize us so we are then ineffective for His (the Lord's) glory.

The disciples were at the beckoning call of Jesus; as His disciples today, should we not be at His beckoning call as well? (No condemnation as there is none for those who are in Christ Jesus (Romans 8:1)…just a challenge).

Our Prayer

Lord, we ask that you will first aid us to trust you more and more so that when you do speak, whether it makes sense or not we will act on what we do know, and that is your voice coupled with our heart of obedience to do *Your* will.

There is so much that we do not understand Lord, but to not understand and to act on *Your* leading requires a trust, that you are guiding us for others to come to experience and know *Your* glory, including us.

Aid us, daily to let go of our intellect so that what makes sense to *You* is accomplished. Healing the broken hearted and setting those who are captive free is *Your* will; aid us to prioritize our will with Yours. Lord, you came to die so that we may live. You came so that not only I, but so that none should perish, and that all would have everlasting life (John 3:16). And You use us to continue to bring about on earth what you died to give.

In Jesus Name, Amen.

Going Deeper:

For Men and Women:

Crazy Love, Overwhelmed by a Relentless God
by Francis Chan

God Chasers
by Tommy Tenney

You Lord Have a Way

You have a way Lord of giving to us the desires of our heart if that desire is aligned with Your will, which is to benefit others and gives You the glory.

The Story

The desire of my heart was to do the post academia of my Master's Degree at a Veteran's administration; this population along with the elderly are who I believe to be a forgotten people.

I was disappointed to the fact that the Veteran's administration accepted only interns who have completed their post-*doctoral* academia.

However, my desire remained…to come to the aid of a Veteran. Just moments ago the Lord fulfilled the desire of my heart in a manner in which I am astonishingly speechless.

As a clinician in the field of mental health at a correctional facility, I had the honor of coming to the aid of a Veteran (there were many; the breach of confidentiality will not exist here). I will never be able to express to you the degree of his pain seen so clearly in his eyes with that of my own. It was a pain so deep that it stifled his ability to speak.

When one lives so long with a terminal kind of emotional pain, without processing it, he or she becomes "accustomed" to it. You see, when there is the presence of a continual pain, coupled with the manner in which one chooses to "numb" it (through a dysfunctional, self-defeating behavior) it actually becomes bearable (because that person is unable to totally feel the degree of its ill effects to the ratio of its presence). The numbing agent of choice, be it alcohol, drugs, shopping, sex or another diversion, diminishes the effect of the pain, but never the reality of its presence.

This man actually died (emotionally) the day he arrived on the front lines (to save our lives I might add), but continued to live (physically).

As this man lay in the cell, isolated and alone…totally alone…God Himself suddenly showed up…without any warning! Although His presence was unannounced, He was warmly invited and embraced.

The agent He chose to reveal Himself through was the woman with the notebook, pen and official badge clipped to her clothing (This woman was me...my awareness of being used was not yet present...just 'doing the rounds' or so I thought.).

Some may desire the spotlight or a day on the show of Oprah. Not me, here I was in my most desired position... crouched down, speaking through the slit, in an iron door, approximately 4" x 13" to a man who would be receptive to the One and Only Who is way more than able to heal the desperate.

I introduced myself to this man and asked him how I could help him. He began to cry and told me his story of how life has never been the same since he returned from the war, and he did not know how to return to the place he was before the aftermath.

I wept.

He wept.

We prayed.

I always, without exception, give each and every person I see inspirational readings about God; however he was in a part of the jail which restricted this intervention. I specifically inquired of the sergeant on duty for permission to do so; my request was granted, and I administered a high dose of God in written form.

I visited him the very next morning; he was crying and crying; I inquired.

He said, "I have read over all the material you gave me over and over again. I feel so much better!" This man was smiling excessively; he could not stop. Looking into the brightness and life in his eyes, I wept in gratitude to the One and only who is able...able to do exceedingly and abundantly more than what we could ask or think (Ephesians 3:20), and that He did!

My Thoughts

Although this man's past residue, from the trauma he endured, did not vanish...he found it; not many do. He found the peace in the pain which is obtainable to all who call upon the Only Name that is above all names, Jesus Christ (Philippians 2:9).

When Christ said that He is an ever-present help in time of trouble (Psalm 46:1) He is a man of His word, because He cannot lie (Titus 1:2). God totally saved this Veteran's life. I did nothing but stand still...completely still, and saw the salvation of the Lord (Exodus 14.13); so did he. When we are clueless we are more likely to be used as a vessel in which the Lord can fill with *His* ways and *His* words, as our mind is not preoccupied with an agenda and wording of our own.

Your Challenge

"To live is Christ and to die is gain" (Philippians 1:21). To live *our* life according to *our*selves is to not live in *His* will. To love the Lord requires obedience to the call of matters that are on

His heart and the manner in which He desires to accomplish them.

In doing this we become less and He becomes greater (John 3:30). Then and only then will we "go about doing good" (Acts 10:38) and be about our Father's business (Luke 2:49).

Oftentimes, more so than not the bound are unseen by the human eye. What holds them captive is encapsulated so deep that their pain is not even at a state of their own consciousness. They are walking in darkness. Ignorance is not bliss.

Great news!

- The darkness shall not overshadow the light (John 1:5).
- Jesus said, "I am the light of the world. Whoever follows me will not walk in darkness but will have the light of life" (John 8:12).
- He also declares, "And I will lead the blind in a way they do not know, in paths that they have not known I will guide them. I will turn the darkness before them into light, the rough places into level ground. These are the things I do, and I do not forsake them (Isaiah 42:16).

Further, what appeared to many as a man confined in a single cell alone, was a man who had just had the greatest day of his life. The walls and the 3" iron door could not bind him; he had been set free, and to us who know the Truth he was set free indeed (John 8:36).

There is someone…somewhere who needs…something. If you are a Christian, you have that something…rather, Someone to offer…Jesus Christ.

Perhaps you are the one, the one who is in need of something (or the presence of someone). Is it peace, courage, wisdom, strength or the assurance that you are not alone?

Whatever your need, He is the "Need-Meeter." He promised to provide for all our needs according to His riches in glory (Philippians 4:19). Surely He has provided for your needs in the past; He is presently and will continue to do so in the future (for the Lord is the same, yesterday, today and forever, Hebrews 13:8). Because He can*not, not* be faithful.

He is unable to do anything else other than remain true to His Word.

If you are a *believer* (in the Lord Jesus Christ) you are called to do just that…BELIEVE! Believe His word (the Bible), and that He is enough all by Himself for any "thing" you are facing or will ever face.

Jesus is the Prince of Peace (Isaiah 9:6). The Prince of the Peace is able to provide Peace in any amount of Pain; He exudes, emits and applies what He is and possesses (a balm like no other…for there is no other able or capable).

When Christ speaks I listen. Wait a minute…what's that Lord? What did you say? "Peace I leave with you; my peace I give you. I do not give to you as the world gives. Do not let your hearts be troubled and do not be afraid" (John 14:27).

Truth (the Word of God).

The therapy of Truth.

The Truth will set you free (John 8:32) as it has for countless others for thousands of years, and will continue to do so as it remains the same…the same wisdom and knowledge which bring about a serene stability.

Our Prayer

Lord, help each one of us to die to our self-serving mission that distorts our vision of what is 20/20 through Your eyes. The pangs of this world create dead men walking. You see them Lord (the hurting); please orchestrate our steps to stand in front of them. Give us eyes to see them; give us ears to hear what the Spirit is saying so we can present You to them.

From our heart of obedience, Your words will speak the only hope they will ever have. "Hope does not disappoint us because God has poured out his love into our hearts by the Holy Spirit, who he has given us" (Romans 5:5).

Thank you Lord for always and forever knowing what is best for us, and for working out on our behalf open doors and closed doors (Revelation 3: 7-8) which bring about the best for our life and in the lives of others.

Lord, there is so much to life; too much oftentimes. We do not understand why things happen or why something does not happen. How do we, in our lack of intellect, resolve a matter that is incomprehensible? Help us all to come to You for we are weary and heavy ladden; only You have promised to give us rest (Matthew 11:28). Rest is in Peace; the peace unattainable elsewhere.

You did not die for no reason at all; You died to give us life and life more abundantly. Lord, we believe...help our unbelief (Mark 9:24).

Pain.

Belief.

Peace.

Rest.

Going Deeper:

For Men and Women:

Come Away My Beloved

by Frances J. Roberts

Streams in the Desert (devotional)

by L. B. Cowman

The Jelly Beans

<u>The Story</u>

You might think this insane, but you ought to know me quite a bit by now!

So…here it goes!

I was at our local library one day, and noticed there were a jar of jelly beans on the counter by the librarian. I thought to myself, "Oh my gosh this is it! It's almost Easter and I bet they want us to guess how many jelly beans there are in the jar!"

Sure enough, in my attempt to find out the protocol, I noticed a sign that stated the age limitation of 12 years and under; being a bit (o.k. 'alotta bit') older *totally* disqualified me!

In my disappointment, I voiced to the Lord, "God, I just wanted to guess how many jelly beans were in there. That's not fair. I wish I could guess how many were in there to enter the contest." (By now you're probably thinking, "What the heck? What's the big deal? Is there a point?")

Well, I thought this was the end of the story; but, I have found out that oftentimes it is not the end of the story until He (the Lord) says it's the end...Little did I know what was to come....

Later that evening I arrived at a very informal Euchre tournament. A friend of mine invited me to *her* friend's home where the competition was. I entered the home I had never been in before, from the attached garage into the owners' kitchen. Immediately upon my entry I....brace yourself...heard a woman scream so excitedly, "Guess how many jelly beans are in the jar and win a prize!"

I looked up; you know what her hands were holding...Yep..."the answer to my prayer."

<u>My Thoughts</u>

You're probably wondering if I won the contest right? No I didn't. But the point here is, I believe wholeheartedly that GOD Himself gave me the desire of my heart...to enter a contest in which I was able to guess the jelly beans!

Crazy? I would say so.

You see God knows precisely what it is going to take to undoubtedly usher in the realness of His presence, and He does it in a manner that lavishes His love on us so the reality of His existence is undeniable.

Coincidence you say? I think that's what I heard you say.

Coincidence defined by *The American Heritage Dictionary* is, "A combination of accidental circumstances that seems to have been planned or arranged." I totally agree and disagree, at the same time. Come let us reason together (Isaiah 1:18).

I must disagree with the former part of the definition of "accidental circumstances." You see Matthew 5:48 declares our heavenly Father is perfect; therefore, we know "perfect" does not bring about "accidental." We are talking "Truth Therapy" here; for believers, the Word of God is the Truth, and that was just…the Truth (the Word of God).

On the other hand, the latter part of "circumstances… planned or arranged" is what I daily live to see (and do see almost daily). Friends who truly know me here the stories, again, almost every single day of my life; they are familiar with many unexplainable events in which I am blessed to experience. These people are brilliant; almost all of them are professionals. They are able to testify to these "unexplainables" which are only defined by no other means than God Himself showing up; the frequency of them is too often.

The Lord granted the desire of my pastor's heart and gave him the color-coordinated 'clip' for his phone by a man at the airport who had the same phone and the opposite color of the clip (See prior story, *The Clip)*. Coincidence? To surmise another avenue of a source is to dismiss the depth and meaning of the intent, and the One who brought it about.

What about *The Button* (also mentioned as a prior story). The Lord went above and beyond and granted the desire of my heart. In order to do this the 'not so old' stereo had to malfunction immediately so my warranty would cover the installment of a new stereo, and therefore acquire the *new* button. By the way, my request was granted within two hours as my stereo was working just fine in the parking lot of my doctor's office; after my appointment, I returned to the car. The cd should have played immediately and did not...the result: a broken stereo and my request for a new button granted simultaneously...a means of provision for the desire of my heart... a new button.

And then...Jelly beans!

Jelly beans on top of all of this (not including the other hundreds of stories I can tell, literally).

You see the Lord desires to:

◆ Draw all men unto Himself (John 12:32); He does this by lavishing us with his love (I John 3:1), and assuring each one of us with the realness of His presence.

Only He knows what it is going to take to turn our gaze to His heart which orchestrates undeniable events through His hand.

Your Challenge

Oftentimes, research is performed for the betterment of humanity.

Why not conduct your very unofficial research study and ask God for something that is only known to Him and you? Why not? I am sure you would agree, you have nothing to lose. (Just make sure your heart is pure before Him; meaning ask Him to forgive you for any sin you have committed because a Holy God can not succumb to unholiness in any manner). Then ask.

Oftentimes in my own life I apply another Truth: We have not because we ask not (Matthew 7:7).

MOST IMPORTANTLY...I am not in any way comparing God Himself to a Genie. Do you desire a Mercedes or winning the multi-million dollar lotto? Not too sure about those things...start with little things and see what happens.

You see, God knows *what* to give us and *when* to give it to us. He will not give to 'ruin us,' but rather to only draw us unto him (Kicking and screamed and throwing a temper tantrum and demanding our own way is not that of humility, but rather that of a spoiled rotten child, and that He does not desire to create.). So great is the love the Father has lavished on us that we should be called children of God (I John 3:1).

Our Prayer

Lord, all throughout Your Word You continually brought about the miraculous. You are the same today as You were then and will forever remain the same for all our tomorrows (Hebrews 13:8). In Your Word You continually astonished others to draw them unto Yourself. That is the ultimate desire of Your heart...to have a deep and meaningful relationship with each one of us; You died to bridge that gap. It is my desire to believe; I pray you help my unbelief (Mark 9:24). I am asking specifically that you _____ (insert a little and meaningful desire of yours for the Lord to bring about). The ultimate desire of my heart is to experience You to a point that it astonishes me, and so that I can tell others of the miraculous brought about by none other than Your mighty, righteous right hand. It is not, in anyway, to manipulate you or to use You for my own gain; again it is only for me to come to know the realness of the One whom sometimes I doubt even exists. I'm sorry Lord for my doubt; it is honesty you desire most, and it is my heart that is being poured out. Help me Lord. Help me to believe. In Jesus Name, Amen.

<u>Going Deeper:</u>

For Men and Women:

Crazy Love, Overwhelmed by a Relentless God
by Francis Chan

National Day of Prayer an Unexpected,
but Welcomed Visitor on the Way to the Pole

<u>The Story</u>

Since 2003 God has laid Flint, Michigan on my heart. This geographical location wrestles with other cities and states within our nation as being the most violent city in America.

Nine years later, May 1, 2012 was National Day of Prayer. "My" idea was to rise early and be at the flagpole, before sunrise, in Flint, Michigan in order to pray for our city (as others across our nation meet).

I had woke up late, and had a very hard time trying to figure out what to wear; not even once a year do I try clothes on and change them over and over again, but this morning was four times of changing my attire before heading out the door. While attempting to find something to wear I realized how absurd this was and the rarity of this occurring...I thought for sure it was

Satan delaying me until…I arrived downtown Flint and was crossing the street at 8:15 a.m.

It was rush hour, and the attempt to get to the other side of the street was quite an ordeal. When I arrived on the sidewalk in front of city hall, a *very* homeless looking girl appeared in front of me (this was apparent by her lack of hygiene and the upheaval of her clothing). This woman was exasperated. She said, "I was so worried about you; I thought you were going to get hit."

"Awww, you're so sweet; thank you," I replied.

I noticed her ball cap; it was black and had white lettering of FLINT. I said to her, "I like your hat, do you love Flint?" "I love Flint," she said. I told her that today was National Day of Prayer, and that I was going to the flagpole to pray. She stated that she was Catholic. I said, "Hay, you have the same God I do." Then what was about to happen happened. She said, "Can I pray with you?" At that very moment I thought, "There is no other place in the whole entire world I would rather be than here in the most violent city in America with a homeless woman whose heart is turned toward the Lord." Divine appointments are what I live to see come about; funny thing is you never know when they are about to come.

I spread my blanket and my Bible in front of the flagpole; we sat down. Immediately she began to cry and cry. I let her cry until she began to catch her breath, and then I said, "Tell me the story." She said, "My mother died two months ago in my arms

120

and I held her as she took her last breath." She continued, "I'm a heroin addict, addicted to Klonopin…[she mentioned some other drugs, and then continued]…I'm a fugitive from Ohio." She immediately showed me a picture of her fiancé. I've seen some mean looking men before but never have I seen one to this degree…ever! This woman was still crying. I touched her on her shoulder and said, "Can I pray for you?" "Yes," she wept. I held up my left hand to the Lord and my right was on her left shoulder. I prayed and prayed and she wept and wept and I did the same. She then began praying for the City of Flint, the inmates at the jail and that God would heal our City.

When we were finished praying, she asked if she could use my phone to see if her social security check went into her bank account; "Sure," I said. Upon hanging the phone up, she was elated for the money was deposited. Then she asked to use my phone again to call her fiancé and tell him the money was in the bank; again I said, "Sure." Then it was if earth stood still. She looked at me as if she had just woke up from a stupor and said, "No…no, if I call him, he'll take all my money; I think it's about time I start taking care of myself." She never called him.

She walked away; out of my care and into the One who is able (Jesus Christ).

My Thoughts

You know it's God when…there is no other place in the whole world that you would rather be than in the most violent city in America with a homeless woman…worshiping God together at a flagpole! Totally out of the box!

I had a plan, and that was to be at the flagpole before sunrise. I felt guilty leaving my home late. I believed my obsessively focused behavior pertaining to my choice of attire was self-centered and a diversion from Satan himself. Ah! Little did I know God had a plan and I had no idea I was walking in it. You see I would have missed that broken heart if I had operated in *my* timing. Oh yes man plans his way, but the Lord orders his steps (Proverbs 16:9). You see I was precisely on time, in His perfect time to the split second. If this woman would had walked past where I was crossing the street, she would have never seen me struggling to get to the other side. Just a split second of time, perfectly orchestrated by the One and Only Who is able to precisely time His will to come about… for His glory!

Peace. Peace in the Pain; I saw it, and she experienced it!

BY *Mary Jo Danyluk*

<u>Your Challenge</u>

Simply…pray and ask the Lord to give you eyes to see and ears to hear what the Spirit is saying; to miss Him is to miss the desire of His heart to be orchestrated *through* you.

He has an agenda and is searching for one to willingly heed His direction by your heart of obedience. Why does He do this? So others can come to experience and know the intimacy they are hungering for so desperately. I will guarantee that you and the one who God set you up with will be totally astonished.

Perhaps you're thinking…Me? Relax. You do not have to do one thing…not one thing. He does it all! It's amazing. God alone had each one of us living and moving and having our being in Him. When it is all of Him…trust me, there is none of us. Perhaps because He is so big, He needs all the room He is given. You see (Here comes the Truth again.) when we become less, He becomes greater (John 3:30).

If you are still saying, "Oh, I…..not me…," you are the furthest away from the truth. All that God desires is a willing heart to be used by Him, and that is it; there are no other pre-requisites…none. And what do you have to do? Pray; nothing else…absolutely nothing. Because in Him we live and move and have our being (Acts 17:28). So let's pray.

<u>Our Prayer</u>

Lord, we ask that You will plainly sharpen our vision to see the plan you have on *Your* heart which needs to be accomplished *through* us (not *by* us), for the benefit of others. Keenly open our ears to hear the manner in which You desire to bring about Your will. The wounded Lord are walking. Our commitment to be Your hands and feet are enmeshed with the desire of Your heart, and that is to heal the broken hearted and to set those who are held captive free (Psalm 147:3). There is a reason why You instructed us to weep with those who weep and to rejoice with those who rejoice (Romans 12:15). There is something about the like-mindedness of heart that occurs which aids in healing. Here we are Lord, send us (Isaiah 6:8). In Jesus Name, Amen.

<u>Going Deeper:</u>

For Men and Women:
It's Not About Me
by Max Lucado

The Lights in the Rear-View Mirror You Never Want to See, but Welcome Whole-Heartedly

<u>The Story</u>

In the past I have accelerated beyond the speed limit an innumerable amount of times; so much so I was sick and tired of being pulled over. In approximately the summer of 2000 I was on my way to church. I was speeding because I did not want to miss one word of my Sunday school teacher.

I had prayed so many times before, "Lord, as soon as I begin to speed remind me to slow down." I had not prayed this in a while and soon noticed lights in my rearview mirror. I pulled over; the police officer met me at the open driver's side window of my car. I immediately said, "I know, I know, I was speeding. You need to give me a ticket please." I continued, "You see, I speed all the time, and I asked God to remind me to slow down so I don't speed." The officer's reply to me was, "Looks like He forgot to remind you this time."

He provided to me what I requested…my ticket. I told him that if I did not suffer the consequence of my behavior, I would just do it again. (He thought I was nuts; at this moment perhaps you do too, but it worked.)

OH…BUT THERE'S ANOTHER STORY…A SEQUEL ABOUT THE LIGHTS IN THE REAR VIEW MIRROR…AGAIN YOU SAY? HERE YOU GO…

<u>A Story of the Like</u>

A very good friend of mine told me of a Christian conference in another state; she stated that I "had" to go. My friend has made many declarations like this in the past, and when she does I know it is God speaking through her; I always go and am always astonished by what God reveals.

I knew the drive from Michigan to this state was approximately six hours so I set myself up to enjoy the ride. I packed about 75-80 Christian cd's; I was looking forward to six hours of "non-stop God!"

When I entered the first freeway around the corner from my home, I committed to ensuring the cruise was set so I would never have to worry about going even one mile over the speed limit; I did this the entire trip. During my travel I noticed the speed limit fluctuating and I adjusted my cruise to the limits.

When…all of a sudden I see police lights in my rearview mirror. I immediately looked at my speedometer. Phew! I thought, he's not pulling me over; my cruise was set and I am still traveling at 70 mph. He kept following me; I then began to wonder if indeed maybe he was pulling me over, but then I saw something. In my rearview mirror I saw the officer behind me *look behind him*; he began to motion with his arms for the car *behind him* to pull over; it was a small red car. At this point I knew beyond a shadow of a doubt that this officer was not pulling me over for: I was not speeding, and He was pulling the man over behind him. The officer was *still* following me. I pulled over. He began screaming at me.

I was shaking and almost began crying. I attempted to inform him that my speedometer reflected a speed of 70 mph; he would not allow me speak *at all*. I was unable to even pronounce the first syllable of "off"-i-cer out of my mouth.

For just a moment I thought, "Maybe my speedometer is off and I was actually speeding, unknowingly. I took my car to have the speedometer checked; they provided me with a Certificate of Accuracy that stated that when my speedometer was registering 70 mph, I was actually driving at a rate of 69 mph.

I decided to fight the ticket and drove another six hours to the state jurisdiction with my certificate to make this wrong a right. I *knew* that *God knew* I was not speeding and that He would be my defense. I took the stand and told my story, the whole truth and nothing but the truth and presented my certificate.

The officer who issued the ticket was present; he took the stand stating the same oath of truth; every word that came out of his mouth was a lie (under oath). He stated that I was vulgar to him and would not stop screaming; in essence he lied. Justice did not prevail.

As I walked to the car I said, "Lord, there is something you want me to learn; what is it?" Immediately, from the time I walked out of the building and into my car, the Lord began to teach me many reasons why this unfolded in my life; they are voiced below.

My Thoughts

After the Lord taught me why all this happened, He told me to write a letter to the officer who ticketed me and lied under oath. God further instructed me to send it registered mail, and that I did. *Below is the content of the letter...word for word.*

Dear (name omitted to protect the officer's dignity):

I want to first of all ease your mind regarding the content of this letter. It is all good-very good. I want to tell you what I have learned.

√ ~I have learned that when I face fear, I must face it and not cower from it (to be honest I was scared to face you).

√ ~I have learned that no matter how much it costs and the time that it takes to do right I must do it.

√ ~I have learned that as long as I stay true to an oath I take to tell the whole truth it is "I" (all of us) that will one day answer to One greater than us, and to stand before Him with clean hands and a pure heart is the desire of my life.

√ ~I have learned that the real reason why I drove to [this state] is so that I can practice not allowing people that have hurt me to become "bitter-makers" in my life.

√ ~Since the moment you pulled me over in [this state] I have not stopped praying for you, and I will continue to do so.

Thank you for teaching me all these things that I would not have ever learned elsewhere.

Very Sincerely,
Mary Jo Danyluk

P. S. If I have done anything to hurt or offend you, please forgive me.

O. K. by now you're probably saying, "You have got to be kidding me?" You also probably even know me quite a bit more by now and assuredly are aware that I am not (kidding).

Your Challenge

Your challenge is the same I was faced with, and that is to set aside our intellect that never operates in the realm of where God is. He stated that He would show us great and mighty things that we know not (Jeremiah 33:3).

Our part is to ask what it is that He wants us to learn.

Sometimes I still think of this experience and pray for the officer. For some reason I believe that we will either meet again or that I was an answer to his mother's prayer for him to come a little closer to God Himself. I believe this as I believe that God is also teaching him something that He would have not learned elsewhere also, but that it is taking him a little longer to get the picture…we'll see. (Maybe that will be in the next book.).

Our Prayer

Lord, our prayer is oftentimes "Why God, why?" We believe that things should just work out in the manner that we believe they should. We think we 'got it going on'…believing we *understand it all (according to our perception)*; when in essence you do have a time, a season and a purpose for everything under heaven (Ecclesiastes 3:1). Help us to walk by faith (the manner in which You see things) rather than by sight (the distortions from our limited view).

Teach us how to understand and accept that which we experience in life; that it is what *You* allow to happen to us for our benefit. Again Your promise says that You will work all things out for our good (if we love you and are called according to your purpose, Romans 8:28). Either You *are* in control of *all* things or You *are not,* and we know better. Straddling the fence hurts us and hinders us to not live in the freedom that You died to give us. Thank you for loving us despite our need to want to control things. Help us to let go and let You be God. In Jesus Name, Amen.

<u>Going Deeper:</u>

For Men and Women:
How to Handle Adversity
    by Charles Stanley
The Necessity of an Enemy
    by Ron Carpenter, Jr.

The Reason for What Season?

<u>The Story</u>

As I sat on my deck tonight I thought of my day, and immediately I saw the faces before me...the Veteran at the jail that God gave me the honor to weep with, the student tonight at the college in which I teach who *so desperately* needs anyone who will listen to him. There is another student who is a mother taking 16 credit hours, and giving it all she has to maintain her honor role status.

I weep with the recollections. Weep in sorrow? Oh my dear, no. Weep because I believe the highest honor that the Lord could give to me is to come alongside so many. You see He has entrusted me those who are the dearest on His heart; that is 'people' who are so dear to His. It is just like having your only child who you have never left in the care of another, and have found that one special person to whom you trust with your child's life.

Again, you see, each one of us has our own reasons why we exist.

Mine is to be at the beckoning call of the One who rewards me with results that have a far more lasting effect…eternity in the hearts of man. And so you say, "What a responsibility! I wish that God would use me like that." My dear if you accept….

The Challenge

There is a reason…there is a reason why we live. Think about it just for one moment…has it been one minute yet? If not then *please* just stop; stop for one moment and think. What is it that you live for? Is it for your children? Your grandchildren? Your clients at work? The weekends? Whatever it is, if it is something or someone other than God Himself it is a chasing after the wind.

Ecclesiastes 3:1 declares, "There is a time for everything, and a season for every activity under the heavens."

Ask Solomon; you have to wait until you get to heaven to do that (in the meantime, read the book of Ecclesiastes in the Bible).

He was the richest man in the world and then realized that all that he had was not what he truly needed. He came to find that *nothing* mattered or satisfied but the presence of God in his life….not presents.

<u>Our Prayer</u>

Lord, we ask you to direct our path to one, only one person that needs Your help to overcome whatever is hindering him or her from experiencing the totality of who You are. We understand that it is not by our might, nor by our power but Your Spirit (Zechariah 4:6); this not only aids others to come to You, but also compels us to clear our agenda so that Yours may reign in and through us. I believe there may be a time when another's life may depend on you coming to them. Please do whatever it takes for us to clear our agenda mentally and spiritually and be devoted to a higher cause than ourselves…and that would be You so that Your glory will not only astonish us but the receiver of your glory as well. Oh how we will be careful to give you all the glory! In Jesus Name, Amen.

Going Deeper:

Crazy Love, Overwhelmed by a Relentless God
by Francis Chan
Growing Strong in the Seasons of Life
by Charles R. Swindoll

Concluding....

Someday You Will be in the Middle of Something or Somewhere

One time I was complaining to God about many things; He told me to look all around as I was sitting in the middle of the woods. I did and there was nothing...anywhere but trees. He said to me so clearly, "In the middle of anything, there I am." Meaning in the middle of any situation...there He is.

My prayer is that you may you come to know, even more than at this moment, a depth of God that you have never experienced. There will forever remain more for us to obtain...an inexhaustible supply. In this day-by-day awakening, I pray as you embrace the attainable (the healing balm of Christ's love) that you realize it is as an opportunity to embark on a part of the Comforter who you would never have otherwise come to know.

Yes. There will forever be pain, but by far…there will forever remain Peace in the Pain as there will forever be God.

The End

I believe now is the time. Now is the time to 'do' something different so the *something different* will happen. The decision time has now come for you to choose to partake, or not, of this remedy to aid you to "have life, and have it more abundant and full" (II Corinthians 9:8).

Christ died so that you yourself can begin to experience the Truth of Who He is, and His ability to aid you to overcome anything and everything.

Praying His will in your life as you seek His face, and come to know the One and only hand that is able to heal.

Is it, at this time, your time? Time to accept and not reject the gift of God Himself. In the gift of God is a new life. Are you ready? Are you ready to give up the old of what has not been working and interject the new?

You see Christ Himself said that He died so that we would not perish but have everlasting life (John 3:16). He has said, old

things are passed away, behold all things become new
(2 Corinthians 5:17).

Different can be embraced, enjoyed and yearned for, because
there is always more to receive…the joy, the constant never
ending Peace in any and all Pain.

He died so you my dear may live…more abundantly…oh so
much *more* abundantly. He Himself has said, "I have come that
they may have life and have it more abundantly" (John 10:10).
"Now unto Him who is able to do immeasurably more than all
we ask or imagine, according to his power that is at work within
us" (Ephesians 3:20).

I ask you Lord to do what is impossible for me and only
possible for You. Please aid this person to make the best decision
as I present the reality of their life before their very eyes.

The Truth

- **For all have sinned and come short of the glory of God (Romans 3:23).**

- **For the wages of sin is death; but the gift of God is eternal life through Jesus Christ our Lord (Romans 6:23).**

- **That if thou [you] shall confess with thy mouth the Lord Jesus and shalt believe in thine heart that God hath raised him from the dead, thou shalt be saved [saved from going to hell] (Romans 10:9).**

I tell you the truth, whoever hears my word and believes him who sent me [that would be me] has eternal life and will not be condemned; he has crossed over from death to life (John 5:24).

So let's do it; let's make sure we see each other one day in heaven.

The scripture says, "For whosoever shall call upon the name of the Lord shall be saved" (Romans 10:13). Let's call on Him. I promise with all that is in me, you have nothing to lose and only beauty to gain.

Ready?

Dear Lord,

I know I have sinned. I believe that God so loved the world that He gave us His only begotten Son, that whosoever believes in Him should not perish, but have everlasting life (John 3:16).

I believe. Please forgive me for all my sins. Help me to live a life that You desire and have planned for me. You have said Lord that, You know the plans you have for me, plans to prosper me and not harm me, to give me a hope and a future (Jeremiah 29:11). Again, I believe. Lead me down the path You have laid just for my life and for Your glory to be revealed in the hearts of many.

In Jesus Name, Amen.

Please email me at:

info@peaceinthepain.com or heisalwaysfaithful@yahoo.com

if you have just placed your life in the hands of Jesus Christ, the

Giver of Life...here and now and in the now to come (heaven).

~~~~~~~~~~~~~~~~~~~~~

"Come unto Me, all who are heavy ladden

and I will give you rest."

(Matthew 11:28)

~~~

"Come and see what God has done,

how awesome his works in man's behalf."

(Psalm 66:5).

~~~~~~~~~~~~~~~~~~

Also email me with "Your Story" in the format in which these

stories were written; perhaps a sequel is in order. Every single

one of us has a story; it is time to give Him the Glory!

If you just so happened to be in a box and the Lord has broke

your Box perhaps it is now time to do what you have longed to

accomplish.

Perhaps it is time for you to take a leap of faith (with no risk)

and write *your* book. Just a thought.

BY *Mary Jo Danyluk*

Ethical/Unethical

~~~~~~~~

What has been hidden shall be hidden no more!

For to harbor a new-found knowledge

beneficial to others

would be for many to suffer great harm...needlessly!

~~~~~~~~

Variances.

Just as variances in the medical field affect one's physical health so do they as well in the state of another's mental health (in the arena of psychology).

In essence, administering the most effective method therapeutically is to likewise state it to be highly ethical as well as scientifically substantial in nature. On the other hand, to withhold such treatment would swing the pendulum to the opposite end of the spectrum.

Thus, the reason for my compulsion; to express verbally in written word a remedial method of intervention into the mental health field (as well as into those whose hearts ache from the everyday pangs of life).

This approach, Truth Therapy: although perhaps widely utilized in every country world-wide, I believe it has not been brought forth to the forefront in the arena of Psychology as an

145

effective treatment option to the depth I believe it should be exposed.

Defined, Truth Therapy is the administration of the Word of God as a tool of intervention to illuminate and overcome the repercussions rooted from an imperfect world, inflicted to imperfect people, by imperfect people.

Through my observations, I have witnessed first-hand, the analysis of variances between the application of spirituality verses the withholding of the same in others' lives.

Assuredly the following individual would confirm my findings as well. He, Dr. Harold Koenig, acquired his undergraduate studies at Stanford University, his medical school training at the University of California in San Francisco. These accomplishments coupled with his study of geriatric medicine, psychiatry and biostatistics training at Duke University Medical Center all culminate to his life's dedication: the study of the presence of spirituality and health with the correlation of positive outcomes in an individual's mental and physical being. Dr. Harold Koenig's 76-page Curriculum Vitae includes hundreds of journals confirming astonishing outcomes when utilizing spirituality in one's life.

I believe the substance within most all secular theoretical approaches to psychology benefit others; however, I state (again first handedly) that the *additional* application of the Word of

God (spirituality) produces benefits that far outweigh the absence of the same.

As an example, the following chart, although not all-inclusive, portrays the correlation of current secular theoretical approaches to the Word of God.

Theoretical Approach	Word of God
Psycholanalytic/Psychodynamic Theory which emphasizes the effects stemming from childhood experiences on the whole of an adulthood person.	"When I was a child, I spake as a child, I understood as a child, I thought as a child: but when I became a man, I put away childish things" (1 Corinthians 13:11).
Cognitive Behavioral Therapy This theory is the basis of our thinking (whether positive or negative) and how each affects our behavioral outcomes to be that of the same nature (positive or negative). It challenges the individual's negative, self-defeating thoughts into that of a more rational and positive nature and thus experiencing positive life changing results.	"For as a man thinketh in his heart so is he..." (Proverbs 23:7).
Humanistic psychology stresses the manner in which an individual behaves is conducive to his/her feelings and view of one's self.	"Therefore if any man be in Christ, he is a new creature: old things are passed away: behold, all things are become new" (2 Corinthians 5:17), and "Remember not the former things, neither consider the things of old" (Isaiah 43:18).

As you have seen in the context of the pages within, scripture was applicable in each story. So it is I believe with *any* situation one may experience in life.

The Truth.

The Truth is the Word of God, and it is the Truth that sets us free (John 8:32).

Free from the pangs of pain, there is peace...always and forever; for there will always be God.

Praying you come to know the depth of the Father (God), His Son (Jesus) and the Holy Spirit who Jesus said would lead us and guide us into all Truth (John 16:13).

~~~~~~~

Where the presence of Truth is
is the application of Peace
and the diminishment of pain.

~~~~~~~~~~~~~~

About the Author

*Mary Jo Danyluk, MAC, LLP*C holds a Master's Degree in Counseling and is a State licensed Counselor.

Also to her credit is her work as an instructor at a nearby college educating students in the arena of Psychology and Social Psychology. She has counseled inmates for years in the jail of one of the most violent cities in America, thereby administering the truths found within Peace in the Pain, and is still witnessing the positive, life changing effects of the administration of Truth Therapy. Her purpose and passion in life are to see others come to an awareness of that which holds them captive, and begin to live a life of freedom based on the Truth.

CONTACT

Mary Jo Danyluk, MAC, LLPC
www.peaceinthepain.com ♦info@peaceinthepain.com
or heisalwaysfaithful@yahoo.com
www.facebook.com/peaceinthepain
(810) 908-2006

Please include your testimony or help received from this book.
Your prayer requests are welcome.

SPEAKING ENGAGEMENTS

CONSULTING

BOOK SIGNINGS

COUNSELING
(One-On-One or Group Therapy Sessions)

Ordering of **Peace in the Pain**/Follow your favorite authors
www.zoelifepub.com